PALESTINIANS AND THEIR SOCIETY 1880–1946

PALESTINIANS AND THEIR SOCIETY 1880–1946

A Photographic Essay

Sarah Graham-Brown

QUARTET BOOKS

LONDON   MELBOURNE   NEW YORK

First published by Quartet Books Limited 1980
A member of the Namara Group
27 Goodge Street, London W1P 1FD

ISBN 0 7043 2225 0 (hardcover)
    0 7043 3343 0 (paperback)

Designed by Namara Features Ltd
Typeset by BSC Typesetting Ltd, London
Printed in England by Shenval '80', Harlow, Essex

Contents

Acknowledgements   vi
Chronology   vii

Introduction   1
Maps   32, 33
1 Land and Village Life   35
2 Villages and the Wider World   73
3 The Bedouin   83
4 Moving Around   89
5 The Economy of Cities and Towns   99
6 Changing Lifestyles   133
7 The Political Scene: War, Politics, Religion   157

Photographic credits   182
Bibliography   183

Acknowledgements

I would like to thank all the people who helped in collecting the photographs for this book. In particular, gratitude to the staff of the Middle East Centre in Oxford, for putting up with the numerous demands I made on their time and expertise – especially to Diana Grimwood-Jones and Gillian Grant, who successively administered the photographic collection from which many of my selections came; and the librarian, Derek Hopwood, for his help and co-operation.

Equal thanks go to George Hobart, of the photographic section of the Library of Congress in Washington – who by his helpfulness during my all too short visit made my encounter with the vast collection of Eric Matson's photographs so fruitful. Also many thanks to friends on the West Bank for their patience and interest and their help in finding photographs I would never otherwise have discovered. In particular, thanks to Salim Tamari and Rita Giacaman in Ramalla and Vera Ṭamari in Amman who spent time helping me track down photographs, cameras and other necessities at short notice.   Also Mrs S. Abboushi, and Sari and Suhad Abboushi for their kind hospitality in Jenin and for taking me to see other families who kindly showed me their collections. I only wish I could have spent more time looking at the wealth of material and historical interest these visits revealed.

Gratitude also to Sina Mansur in Ramalla for letting me use her family photographs and telling me of their history and to her husband who let me see and use the archive of the Quaker Girls School in Ramalla.

As for the actual writing of the book, it would not have been completed without support and encouragement from many friends whom I also have to thank for listening to my ideas and contributing suggestions and advice.

Most special thanks, however, go to the people who read the finished manuscript and gave searching and constructive criticism – Barbara Smith, Libby Grimshaw and Jonathan Mirsky. Their help was invaluable.

Finally, my thanks go to the people I have worked with at Quartet Books, particularly Roy Trevelion, for allowing me to help with the book's design and for his imagination and skill in dealing with a complicated layout.

Chronology

1897	First Zionist Congress meets in Basle, Switzerland.
1898	Kaiser Wilhelm of Germany visits Jerusalem.
1908-9	Young Turk revolution in Istanbul. Sultan Abdul Hamid deposed.
1911-13	Ottomans fight a series of wars in the Balkans.
1913	First Arab nationalist congress meets in Paris.
1914 (August)	World War I begins.
1916 (May)	Sykes-Picot agreement on partition of the Ottoman Empire signed in London by British and French representatives.
1916 (June)	Uprising in the Hijaz (Western Arabia) against the Turks led by the Sharif of Mecca and his sons with British assistance.
1917 (November)	Balfour Declaration pledging Britain to establish a national home for the Jews in Palestine.
1917 (November)	British troops under General Allenby occupy Jerusalem.
1918 (October)	Damascus captured by British and Arab forces. Amir Faisal (one of Sharif Hussain's sons) becomes *de facto* ruler.
1919	Versailles Conference of post-war settlement.
1920 (April)	Mandate system approved at San Remo Conference. Palestine designated as one of the mandated territories.
1920 (April)	Anti-Zionist riots in Jerusalem during the Muslim festival of Nebi Musa.
1920 (July)	French occupy Damascus and Amir Faisal is forced out.
1920 (July)	Sir Herbert Samuel, first British High Commissioner for Palestine, arrives in Jerusalem.
1921 (May)	Anti-Zionist riots in Jaffa after clashes during May Day demonstrations between different sections of the Jewish labour movement.
1929	Wall Street crash. Beginning of world trade recesion.
1929 (August)	'Wailing Wall' riots in Jerusalem and attack by Arabs on the Jewish quarter in Hebron leaving sixty Jews dead.
1930 (October)	British White Paper on policy in Palestine following reports on the 1929 riots by the Shaw Commission and the report on the condition of Palestinian agriculturalists by Sir John Hope Simpson. The White Paper caused an outcry in Zionist circles because it called for restrictions on Jewish immigration into Palestine.
1931 (January)	Letter from Ramsay Macdonald, the British Prime Minister, to Zionist leader Chaim Weizman reaffirming Britain's commitment to the National Home policy. This was dubbed the 'Black Letter' by Palestinians who saw it as a reversal of the White Paper's policy brought about by Zionist pressure.
1933	Hitler comes to power in Germany.
1933 (October)	Riots in Jaffa and Jerusalem with strong anti-British overtones.
1936 (April – October)	Arab general strike and rebellion.
1936 (November)	Royal Commission sent out to Palestine to investigate the strike. Partially boycotted by Arab leadership.
1937 (July)	Royal Commission report recommends partition of Palestine into Jewish and Arab states. Strong opposition from Arabs.
1937 (September – end 1938)	Second phase of Arab rebellion.
1939 (February)	Round Table Conference on Palestine in London, followed by 1939 White Paper restricting Jewish immigration and land buying.
1939 (September)	Outbreak of World War II.
1942 (May)	Biltmore Programme issued by the Jewish Agency after a meeting in New York, demanding unlimited Jewish immigration into Palestine and the establishment of a 'Jewish Commonwealth' there.
1946 (January)	Anglo-American commission of enquiry visits Palestine and recommends continuation of the British Mandate.
1946 (September) – 1947 (February)	London Conference on the future of Palestine to consider British proposals for its division into Jewish and Arab provinces under a British High Commissioner. Representatives of some Arab governments attend the conference but no representatives of Palestinian Arabs or Zionists.
1947 (February)	British decision to relinquish the Palestine Mandate.

Introduction

Photographs and History

'The relation between what we see and what we know is never settled' (John Berger, *Ways of Seeing,* Harmondsworth, 1972, p.7)

This photograph was taken in the 1920s or 1930s by one of the most prolific commercial photographers working in Palestine at that time.

It is the kind of photo designed to be reproduced as a souvenir of the 'Holy Land' for pilgrims or tourists (these categories being almost interchangeable). Pictures of this type were, therefore, among the most widely disseminated visual images of Palestine, finding their way into European and North American homes in the form of postcards and glass or stereoscopic slides.

What would a picture like this be a souvenir of? Even if the caption (provided by the photographer) were not there, most European viewers with a smattering of religious and biblical education would not have much trouble in guessing its intended significance. The poses of the subjects are familiar from generations of Christmas cards. But the subjects are *not* 'the Holy Family' of the Bible but a Palestinian peasant family living under British Mandate rule. They may have been a nuclear family but since the photographer has so manipulated the scene to fit the image he required, there is no certainty that the people in the picture are related at all. However, for the photographer creating this particular product, and no doubt for many

1

A Judean home, suggestive of 'the Wise Men seeking the Christ Child' (photographer's caption). Judea refers to the hill region around Jerusalem.

of the consumers, this would be an irrelevant quibble. Their interest was concentrated on the apparently timeless image which converted these people – whose names and histories remain unknown – into something of significance, within a particular religion and culture. To the subjects of the photograph, this meaning might be quite incomprehensible.

This 'Holy Family' may be a particularly crude example of how photographs were turned into biblical allegories, though it is not unusual to find similar allusions made in more or less subtle ways. Nonetheless, the photograph does illustrate one of the more obvious problems of using still pictures as historical evidence of the way society worked.

Another question is how various sorts of stereotypes – visual or otherwise – come to be accepted as 'truths' about a people or a culture. In Palestine, as in most colonised and semi-colonised societies of the nineteenth and twentieth centuries, external forces played a crucial part in shaping events. Such societies were particularly vulnerable to the invention of types to fit supposed characteristics as perceived by their rulers. The ruled were sometimes even persuaded of their validity. One effect was to create an impression of passivity – of a people, the Palestinians for example, to whom history just happened, usually in a rather uncomfortable way. Attempts to resist the march of this 'history' were generally made out to be the result of ignorance or a natural tendency to engage in irrational violence.

The Palestinian problem has now emerged in the public eye as an 'issue', whether reluctantly or willingly acknowledged. Recognition of the 'issue', however, with its connotations both of violence and helplessness, still evades the question of understanding the Palestinians as people with a history and a social structure. It is from these that their present sense of identity has emerged.

1

This book examines some aspects of Palestinian society from the last stages of Ottoman rule (1880) to the final years of effective British control (1945/46), through contemporary photographs taken variously by rulers, ruled and passing observers. It does not pretend to be a scholarly or comprehensive socio-economic history of the Palestinians. The aim is rather to give an impressionistic view of the relation and interaction between a particular nation's social and political history and some of the images which were made of that history.

The book does not deal with the internal history of Zionism or the Jewish community in Palestine either before or during the Mandate except insofar as it affected, economically and politically, the lives of the indigenous Palestinian community. Socially, each community lived more or less separately, with its own preoccupations and forms of organisation.

It may also be asked why the book ends its narrative immediately after World War II. The main reason is that the period from 1946 onwards signalled the end of the era in which Palestinians could take any element of their society or their identity for granted. Their history continued after the dispersion of 1948 but in other places and under greatly changed circumstances. Furthermore, most of the reasons behind the events leading up to the announcement that the State of Israel had come into existence (1948) are not to be found in those last violent moments themselves but in the history of the years which preceded them.

Ideas in the West about Palestinians during the last thirty or so years have been concentrated around two main themes – the hapless and helpless refugee and the gun-wielding guerilla. Since this book stops short of the period in which these new views evolved, it does not attempt to deal with them directly, but many of the assumptions which stand behind the symbols of the UNRWA★ ration card and the Kalashnikov were also implicit in earlier depictions.

We are now so bombarded with photographs and other imagery about our own and other societies that we often absorb them without conscious thought. Visual representation is nonetheless a powerful agent in creating and reinforcing views about the world, particularly about parts of

★United Nations Relief and Works Agency, established specifically to deal with Palestinian refugees.

it which have long been considered by the West as primitive, irrational and changeless. It may be worthwhile confronting some of the past pictures and ideas on which these views were built.

Photographs, like any other form of historical evidence, pose their own particular problems of interpretation. While in some respects they may appear more 'real' than a table of statistics or a document – because they are actual representations of people and places – they can, like statistics, distort as much as they reveal. The historian, equally, will choose what aspect of the column of numbers or the people and objects in the picture to emphasise.

Pitfalls specific to photographic evidence range from the selectivity of the photographer through the way the particular angle of the sun affected what got into a photograph to decisions to crop the finished product so as to focus attention on one aspect of the scene while discarding another. Styles of reproduction can also affect the mood of a photograph – a soft sepia print can produce a calm aura of 'things past' while obscuring material details. Another print in hard-edged black and white may, conversely, convey a sense of harsh 'reality'.

Dating of photographs, or its absence, can depend quite randomly on whether the print or negative one sees has been labelled. On the other hand, it can also be an intentional omission. The Holy Family photograph shown earlier has no date because its purpose – to convey timelessness and to be sold to tourists year after year – would make dating it counter-productive.

With or without dates, the process of re-anchoring these fragmented glimpses of the past in a historical context of narrative or argument is not impossible but like other fragmentary sources of data, inevitably presents problems of interpretation.

Perhaps the most interesting and fruitful aspect of seeking an interpretive framework for these pictures is the interrelation between what material and social evidence can, with reasonable certainty, be gleaned from them and what the photographer thought was captured through his or her lens. While personal and aesthetic tastes and idiosyncracies can never be discounted in this process of selection, nationality, social class and political views also exercised a powerful influence over what was 'seen' and recorded and what was ignored.

3

2

2 3

Two approaches to the same subject – a bread stall in Jerusalem. The first is labelled 'Veiled woman at bread stall', with the interest concentrated on the fact that urban women often wore veils, though it shows other mundane details as well. The second, a postcard with a request on the back to the recipient to 'identify yourself with the Jerusalem and East Mission and help bring again the Christian faith to the Holy Land', has little of the mundane about it, but a good deal of the exotic and melodramatic.

4

*Bonfils: monumental
architecture as a studio
backdrop to jewellery sellers·
posed with their wares.*

The majority of the photographs used in this book are taken by Europeans either for themselves or for a European audience and, leaving aside for a moment the question of the specific labels and stereotypes which would be hung on things Palestinian, there is a more general problem which concerns the portrayal of different and unfamiliar scenes from another culture. Familiarity may not always make for understanding, but certainly *un*familiarity – the inability to comprehend the significance of actions or gestures in another culture – makes it difficult to see them as meaningful or rational. Strangeness may fascinate, or it may call forth other emotions – hostility, fear, contempt, condescension. The camera provides the technology to record not just an object or person but the photographer's perception that it is strange and alien.

A further ingredient has already been mentioned – late nineteenth- and early twentieth-century Europe's view of 'the rest of the world'. The power relationship through which the major European nations manipulated politically and/or economically the destinies of most of the 'rest' of the world predisposed Europeans, as administrators, missionaries or travellers, to view the peoples controlled or influenced by them as not simply strange but decidedly inferior.

This view took a variety of forms. Some applied in a general way to non-European peoples, others had more specific application – for instance, to the 'Orient' or to Palestine.

There are in certain corners of the globe races which have had the unenviable privilege of undergoing no change, not even for the better. *These the historian would like to preserve, for his own purposes, in their archaic integrity, as fields of study, if not of experiment, and as a kind of laboratory in which he could observe at leisure the phenomena of human evolution.* But, unfortunately, or perhaps fortunately, such day-dreams are always destined to be upset by the progress of civilisation, which everywhere, sooner or later, sweeps away the ruins of the past to make room for the future. Palestine, so long spared, is already undergoing the common lot. A strong current of immigration from central Europe has for some time set in upon it, and a few years will do what centuries have not been able to effect.

There is no time to be lost. Already the first note of menace has been sounded, and a projected railway from Jaffa to Jerusalem warns us to make haste and accomplish the laborious task of exploration, and perfect a complete inventory of the historic and scientific treasures of this unique country, before it has been deprived of every relic and memorial of the past. It will be too late when, on the spot where the cry of Rachel mourning for her children still lingers, we hear in mocking echo the shrill scream of the railway whistle, and the loud shout of 'Bethléhem! Dix minutes d'arrêt! Les voyageurs pour la Mer Morte changent de voiture!'

(C. Clermont Ganneau, 'The Arabs in Palestine' in *Survey of Western Palestine: Special Papers on Topography*, London, 1881, p. 315). My italics

Clermont Ganneau worked with the London-based Palestine Exploration Fund which in the course of the 1870s and 1880s produced the most comprehensive survey available for this period on the geography, topography, archaeology, flora and fauna of Palestine. One might gather from the tone of the quotation that he regarded the Palestinians themselves as vital specimens only insofar as they were illustrative of how things must have been two thousand and more years before. Although the survey as a whole meticulously covers the country village by village and biblical site by biblical site, it is noticeable that much more attention is paid to buildings, ruins, water sources and so on than to people as they lived in 1880. The maps which accompanied the text were drawn by the Royal Engineers and bequeathed to the War Office which found them of considerable use in subsequent strategic planning.

The strain of biblical concern coupled with the undertone of growing imperial interest runs through much of the European writing of the pre-World War I era on Palestine.

Clermont Ganneau's remarks also convey a profoundly ambiguous attitude to social and economic change which despises 'backward' and 'archaic' races in Palestine but rails against 'progress' (in this case he refers to Jewish immigration as its bearer) because it upsets the museum-like timelessness which he perceives there.

Edward Said, in his book *Orientalism*, traces some of the cultural and intellectual influences on European views of the Middle East. He shows how the concept of the 'oriental' as a 'type' of humanity has drained persons or groups so labelled of their historical and personal identity. Like the biblical category, the 'oriental' concept takes the subject and its actions out of historical context and makes it appear exotic, inexplicable and not susceptible to rational interpretation. Meaning can only be restored to these scenes by applying to them the generalised concepts developed in European academic circles devoted to the study of the 'Orient'. The exact content of these generalisations varies according to whether they came from France, Britain or Germany but Said describes the confrontation of 'the Orientalist' with 'the Orient' like this:

When a learned Orientalist travelled to the country of his specialization, it was always with unshakable abstract maxims about the 'civilization' he had studied; rarely were Orientalists interested in anything except proving the validity of these musty 'truths' by applying them, without great success, to uncomprehending, hence degenerate, natives. Finally, the very power and scope of Orientalism produced not only a fair amount of exact positive knowledge about the Orient but also a kind of second-order knowledge – lurking in such places as the 'Oriental' tale, the mythology of the mysterious East, notions of Asian inscrutability – with a life of its own, what V. G. Kiernan has aptly called 'Europe's collective day-dream of the Orient.'

(E. Said, *Orientalism*, London, 1978, p. 52)

Another form of labelling in the nineteenth century was the habit of classing people the world over in loosely defined ethnic and racial 'types'. For Palestine the commonest labels were Bedouin, peasant *(fallah)* and townsman. In all parts of Greater Syria (that is from Anatolia in the north to Arabia in the south and eastwards to Iraq) these 'types' were usually assumed to have different racial origins. Adjectives from the 'orientalist' stable helped further to specify how they should be regarded. Bedouin were usually 'wild', 'cruel', 'free' but with a 'code of desert honour', fallahin were archaic, ignorant, naive, oppressed, sometimes defined in contrast to the bedouin as being without 'honour' or 'moral sense'. Townspeople also came in for the latter tag to which was added 'scheming', 'Levantine', 'devious' and 'fawning'.

5

Bonfils: view of a 'bedouin chief' – far away from the clean desert air so praised by T. E. Lawrence and others, posed in the studio in front of a palm tree-painted screen.

6
Cameramen at work during the Maundy Thursday ceremonies
at the Holy Sepulchre Church in Jerusalem before World War
I. One of the two precariously suspended in the centre has his
head under the black cloth hood to exclude light.

The Photographers

Obviously attitudes of this kind rubbed off not just on the sort of captions given to pictures but on the photographers' choice of subject and their manner of presenting it in the finished image, though exactly how they exercised these preferences depended very much on the specific reasons for which they took pictures. Those with a commercial market in mind looked for scenes which they thought would have popular appeal and by so doing reinforced public taste for well tried visual clichés.

Of course, technology also exercised considerable influence over what could and could not be photographed and under what conditions. Eric Matson, who spent some fifty years in Palestine as a photographer, looked back in 1969 to his early techniques.

In the early days, our picture-taking and processing were somewhat primitive and often improvised. We had to sensitize our own albuminized printing paper and used sunlight as our light source. Our earliest enlargements were made by placing a box camera through the window of a darkened room, putting the glass negative of the picture to be enlarged into the camera, and projecting its image, by means of the daylight behind the camera, onto bromide paper that was placed on an easel inside the room at a distance determined by the desired size of the enlargement . . . For a number of years, we used a 'cabinet size' camera for 13 x 18 cm . . . glass plates. The camera had a division fixture and was used for taking stereoscopic views with a double lens. For a full-plate picture, the division was removed and a single lens used. We also used a large plate camera with which our 24 x 30 cm . . . negatives were taken. In later years, after glass plates were generally replaced by films, I used 9 x 12 cm films . . . and, to a lesser extent, the smaller, 6 x 9 cm film packs. . . . In the later years, our cameras included the German Plaubel Machina for press work, the German 9 x 12 cm Voigtlander, Eastman's Graflex, and, for 35 mm the Contax and Leica.

(Quoted in George S. Hobart, 'The Matson Collection: half century of photography in the Middle East' in *Library of Congress Quarterly Journal*, January 1973, Vol. 30, No. 1, pp. 25–26)

7
European tourists watching Russian pilgrims at the Epiphany ceremony of dipping in the Jordan river. The woman on the right is taking a photograph. The introduction of cheap portable cameras in the 1890s made it possible for tourists to create their own photographic souvenirs in addition to collecting commercially produced pictures.

Matson worked for the photographic department of the American Colony in Jerusalem, a small religious colony of Americans founded in Palestine in 1881 by a Chicago lawyer. The colony became quite influential in Jerusalem life and also set up a commercial venture known as the American Colony Stores. This store sold various souvenirs including photographs and slides, many of which were Matson productions. He composed series of biblical scenes, of which 'the Holy Family' shown earlier was an example. In the 1930s he experimented with new techniques – for instance, a striking series of night shots and an early colour photography project for the Royal Geographical Society. As political turmoil became almost a part of everyday life, his camera was turned more and more to these subjects and rather less to the curious and the picturesque which featured prominently in his earlier work. Matson achieved considerable technical competence, and artistic effect clearly became a major preoccupation with him.

More striking examples of the primacy of this motive can be seen in the work of the French photographer, Felix Bonfils who took pictures all over Greater Syria in the mid nineteenth century. His work was even more heavily contrived and constrained by technical limitations than Matson's. Many of his shots of people are taken in studios, with peasants, bedouin and townspeople improbably and often artfully posed against painted backdrops. Many of them were presumably persuaded from the street or the coffee house to be photographed. Such pictures are difficult to use as any guide to dress, artifacts or social behaviour, since all are jumbled to fit the photographer's vision of what would make a good picture.

Another genre of professional photography which appears in this book is straightforward studio portraiture which had no pretensions whatever to naturalism. On the contrary, the subject is usually dressed up, isolated against the studio backcloth, sitting, reclining or propped against desk or tree stump with fixed expression and stiffened limbs. Such portraits are to be found, as they are in many other parts of the world, in the albums and collections of middle- and upper-class Palestinian families and while they seldom give much clue of the personality of the sitter, the style of the picture sometimes indicates the importance of various sorts of social status symbols both in the eyes of the photographer and the sitter. There were by the 1930s a number of local photographers in the large towns who did this kind of work.

Most of the other pictures used in this book were taken by amateurs, some of whom were passing visitors, others who spent longer in the country. In the latter case, particular concerns and interests based on profession, sex and nationality are usually evident.

One fairly large group of photographs comes from missionary sources – the majority British or American, and Protestant. Strictly religious affairs aside, they display more than average interest in education, health and details of village life. This is also a source for material on women – beyond, that is, the type-cast 'peasant girl/bedouin women' shots. Some of the photographers were women and were interested, in one way or another, in what women did: in child rearing, domestic work, crafts and so on. Equally it seems likely that, on the whole, village women would be more willing to be photographed by a woman than by a man.

Recording the present state of things was not always the only intention of these pictures, however. It was also to demonstrate what needed to be changed – in health, education, social behaviour. While there may be no denying that poverty, illness and illiteracy in village life needed to be remedied, there was usually an implicit but clearly predetermined idea about what the remedies should be. This was normally based on the view that these people were backward and childlike and needed to be directed to better paths. The villagers thus become people – in life and on film – to whom and for whom things should be done.

8 9

Stereoscopic slides which, when viewed through a stereoscope, appeared three-dimensional, were very popular in the late nineteenth century and were big business for their publishers, such as, in this case, Underwood and Underwood. The first picture is a visual trick – when seen in three dimensions the smoke from the gun actually appears to be hanging in the air. Note the biblical references – attached as a matter of course.

8

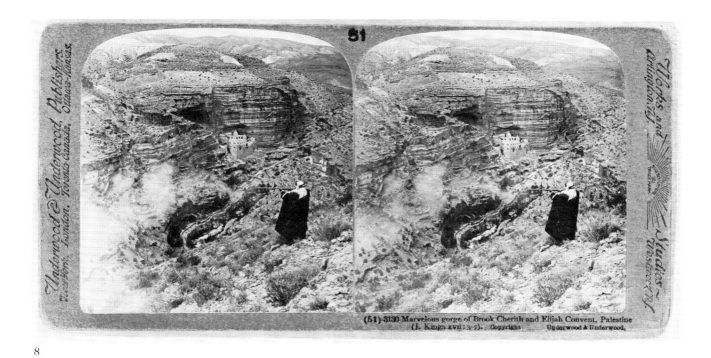

(51)-3130-Marvelous gorge of Brook Cherith and Elijah Convent, Palestine (1. Kings xvii : 3-7). Copyright Underwood & Underwood.

9

(52)-3131-A street in Ramah, Palestine (1 Sam. 1: 19-20). Copyright Underwood & Underwood.

10

*A Bonfils portrait of Syrian
bedouin women, carefully posed.*

11 12

Two studio portraits of children from the Quaker school in Ramalla. The girl has been specially dressed up. The boy clutches a book, symbolic of the importance of education to the people for whom the photograph was taken.

The biblical past was the other focus of interest. Even on photographs of considerable interest for what they show of present life, the temptation to append a supposedly apt biblical quotation to the caption seemed to be overwhelming. This attitude of mind is practically expressed by Frances Newton who worked as a teacher and school supervisor in Palestine for some years.

I had noticed that the tourists eagerly bought up [my] small wooden models of the native plough, and of the pottery jars in which the women fetched water from the Virgin's fountain in Nazareth. I expanded the idea into a series of models, and other articles, illustrating and explaining references in the Bible. By so doing, their inner meaning was unveiled to the eyes and minds of the Europeans. Apart from its commercial aspect, the study and research provided me with a fascinating recreation. I built up quite a good business, with instincts inherited from my banker father.

(Frances Newton, *Fifty Years in Palestine*, London, 1948, p. 39)

Her attitude is in many respects similar to that of Clermont Ganneau, quoted earlier, though without his disdain and alienation. In fact Frances Newton displayed considerable sympathy politically for the Palestinians and wrote strongly against both Zionism and the way the British conducted themselves. She even publicly condemned the behaviour of British forces engaged in punitive action against villages during the 1936-9 rebellions. Nonetheless, even the assertion that Palestinians had a right to continue to live on this particular stretch of land was somehow tied up with their supposed 'biblical' roots. Here is the view of another supporter of the 'Arab cause' at this time. He is contesting the view that the granting by the British of the Rutenberg Electricity Concession (see p. 111) was justified by appeals to 'material progress'.

The obvious destiny of Palestine was to become a nest of smallholdings, of which the smallish external wants would be supplied by the coastal towns.

This was a simple and thoroughly native prospect. It connoted a Palestine suited to the feelings and the customs of the population. It connoted too – this being a point never enough raised – a Palestine in complete accordance with its other, transcendental self, the Holy Land.

(J. M. N. Jeffries, *Palestine: The Reality*, London, 1939, p. 441)

Here we have a fusion between the Englishman's notion of what forms of economic life are appropriate for a native population and the orientalist concept described by Said. The 'meaning' of Palestine, as perceived here, lies essentially in 'the Holy Land' not in the 'nest of smallholders' whose future is benevolently considered.

The albums of British officials display a range of ideas and preoccupations which probably do not differ very greatly from those of colonial officials in other countries as far as attitudes to the 'native' population were concerned. They display the preoccupations of rulers with their subjects – that they should be clean, healthy and less ignorant (as long as this did not cost too much), but more important that they should be docile and co-operative towards the authorities. Paternalism and a heavier handed kind of authority are constantly intermingled. The situation was complicated by the fact that there was another community – the Jewish settlers – not British but European and therefore not classifiable as 'native', whom some of these officials were not at all sure they liked or knew how to deal with. On the other hand (and photographs often reveal this) they usually had an admiration – grudging or otherwise – for the 'modern' aspects of the settlers' endeavours and for their technological progressiveness.

Palestine's Arab inhabitants, by contrast, might be considered photogenic material for tourists and evoked in some officials a paternalist desire to improve their conditions, but their society and economy did not conform with western ideas of progress and dynamism.

13 14

Two different reactions to the camera by women, taken by the same photographer.
Below:
a woman shields her child from the 'evil eye', here presumably represented by the camera, while
Above:
a peasant girl looks straight at the camera and makes a face.

14

13

Village elders and child. No names, village unknown.

What of photographs taken by Palestinians themselves, or at least taken specifically for them? How do they reflect the society's own view of itself?

The first point is rather an obvious one, but it influenced the kind of photographs which were taken. With rare exceptions, those who had cameras themselves, or had photographs taken for their own memory and enjoyment, were reasonably well off, coming from towns large and small. The poor, and those who lived in villages, are seldom so self-recorded. Most photographic images of them are the work of 'outsiders' – either foreigners or towndwellers. The section of Palestinian society which viewed itself through the camera's lens before the mid-twentieth century is therefore relatively limited. Individual portraits and pictures of family gatherings or political events are nonetheless interesting reflections of particular social groups in urban society, and their distinctions of dress and manner. They may also say a good deal about the differing attitudes of various class and religious groups towards European culture. One can also trace through these and other kinds of photographs the influence of nationalist sentiment in changing styles of dress, if not of behaviour. Of family and other relationships which engaged the individuals concerned, photographs can only give the most minimal of indications.

Another important distinction is evident – between photographs of 'notable' people, the rich, the educated and the articulate, whoever took them, and photographs of the poor and illiterate. The former are individuals who have names and therefore identities – whether in captions, or scribbled on the back of the print. The latter are nameless – seldom distinguished except by a label: 'peasant', 'cobbler', 'man on donkey'. This is an inequality in the photographic 'memory' beyond the fantasies, distortions and simplifications already described.

Looking at pictures of a society which has since been destroyed or dispersed is liable to enhance the aura of nostalgia which attaches to dusty photographs dug out of trunks and attics. The Palestinians (without the aid of photographs) have tenaciously preserved the memory of that past, which acts as a form of reinforcement in an unenviable present and a strong assertion of national and personal identity.

However, for a historian, however sympathetic, the temptation to both kinds of nostalgia needs to be resisted, because 'the past' can be then made to seem like a single unchanging entity instead of a constantly changing succession of events and processes. Furthermore, any kind of nostalgia invites the suspension of critical judgement.

Palestinians may be able to restore to themselves a national homeland but their political and social experiences since 1948 preclude restoration of the former social order. Nor, I imagine, would most want it.

Palestinians 'dressed up'.
Below:
*members of a middle-class
Palestinian family who
would usually have worn
European clothes dressed up
in 'traditional' clothes for a
party (1920s).*
Above:
*St George's Anglican School
in Jerusalem, 1907. A
performance of* The
Merchant of Venice, *with
Tawfiq Hussaini as the
Prince of Morocco.*

Power and Social Structure

Brecht once pointed out that a photograph of the Krupp works (the vast German steel empire) reveals virtually nothing about its organisation.

This raises a rather different problem from the ones already described – how photographers manipulate their subjects and authors of photographic books in turn interpret and manipulate the photographs.

There are certain areas quite basic to historical narrative and interpretation which photographs do not reveal, or reveal only by association. Power relationships, for instance, are only obvious when physical coercion is being used – a father beating his child, an overseer driving slave labourers, a policeman dragging away a demonstrator, a tank being driven through curfewed streets. Otherwise visual evidence of power and authority is largely symbolic. Both these forms of evidence will appear in this book, but they are inadequate to interpret the complexities of changing power relationships in Palestine.

Only by juxtaposition or collage can photographs be made to show these aspects of the workings of society. This device can be visually striking and effective but is always in danger of oversimplification. It is therefore necessary here to provide an analysis of those class and power relationships which lie behind the photographs.

At no time during the years covered by this book or, for that matter, since, have Palestinians controlled their destinies through a government of their own choosing. This powerlessness has had both material and cultural effects on their society and political perspectives. Various avenues to power and status have always existed but their scope and effectiveness has almost always depended on external forces.

The most obvious of these 'external forces' were the two imperial powers which ruled Palestine – the Ottomans and the British. They had different reasons for being in Palestine but neither were willing to cede self rule to its inhabitants.

The Ottomans ruled Palestine from 1517 to 1917 as part of a group of provinces with fluctuating boundaries within greater Syria (i.e. from borders of Anatolia in the north to Sinai in the south and east to Iraq)*. From 1831 to 1840 they lost control briefly to the forces of Ibrahim Pasha, son of the rebel governor of Egypt, Mehemet Ali. In the nineteenth century their Empire came under increasing pressure from the major European powers, to which they constantly lost territory and became more and more indebted. As a result, the Ottomans were mainly preoccupied with bolstering the army with new recruits and gathering tax revenues to fill a depleted Treasury. These needs were an incentive to regain more effective control over their Arab provinces than they had achieved in the previous century. In Palestine this was accomplished after the end of the Egyptian occupation, from 1840 onwards, and most areas of the country were subdued by the 1880s.

Taxation and conscription fell proportionally heaviest on the rural population. The main agricultural tax was the tithe – 10% and later 12% of the gross yield of the land. This may not seem very high until one takes into account the fact that tax collectors (who were not government officials) very often took a considerably larger cut by force or threat of force. And government troops were sometimes used in the countryside to back up the tax collectors. Also peasants were often in debt – and frequently to the same person who collected the taxes. In this respect tax franchises *(iltizam)* were often quite profitable – some merchants and landowners who held them built up their fortunes in this way.

After 1860 some attempt was made to reorganise tax collection. By putting it in the hands of government officials rather than tax farmers, it was hoped that more of the money would thereby reach its intended destination. In Palestine, however, this plan did not materialise. In many areas, tax farms were auctioned annually instead of following a hereditary route as they had previously. They had originated as a way of rewarding Ottoman army officers and officials who could pass the right on to their children. But as far as the peasants were concerned the change did not make much difference.

*Note:
The terms Syria, Lebanon, Iraq and Palestine – referring to the entities created after World War I – will for convenience also be used to refer to these areas when they were provinces under Ottoman rule, although the boundaries do not correspond (see map).

The Turkish governor of Nazareth at the turn of the century.

20

Druze from Mount Carmel. The Druze are a sect which split with orthodox Islam, more numerous in Syria and Lebanon than in Palestine but having a distinct identity in both areas. In the nineteenth century the British established themselves as the 'protectors' of the Druze, particularly in Lebanon.

The tithe was one of the most regular and significant ways in which the state intervened in the lives of its subjects. Urban taxes also existed but were on the whole not so onerous, affecting a smaller section of the population and on the whole a better-off one.

Conscription, by taking away able-bodied young men from the labour force, also affected the peasantry more than other segments of the population. Muslims, who formed the majority of rural-dwellers, could not be exempted from military service, as could Christians.

656. Druses du mont Carmel prenant leur repas.   Bonfils

On the whole, the less privileged part of the Palestinian population seems to have viewed the Ottoman state with indifference when they were left alone, but with fear and suspicion when demands were made on them. More was taken away than was given. Ottoman governors of districts and provinces were changed regularly to prevent them from establishing too strong a local power base. They varied greatly in their attitude to their jobs. Whatever they did was more noticeable to those who lived in the provincial town than in the surrounding villages but there were reforming officials who had a reputation for benevolence and could be appealed to against other oppressors. Nevertheless, given the very quick turnover of officials, this situation could never be relied on to last. Benevolence, if it appeared at all, was based solely on individual attitudes rather than imperial policy. Government-inspired reforms were designed not so much to improve their subjects' lives as to make Ottoman rule more effective and to bow to pressures from the European powers for concessions to their (mostly Christian) protégé groups: an example was the so-called Tanzimat era (between the 1830s and 1860s) of attempted reform of the administration, army and economy of the Empire, whose purpose was primarily to forestall further European pressure and interference.

The urban population had rather more regular contacts with government authority. However, the concentration of Christians and also Jews in the towns strengthened the operation of the *millet* system which divided the population along confessional lines and treated each community as a self-regulating entity. This meant that each community would deal with the government through a mediating religious official or notable.

The Ottoman government was, however, not the only political or economic influence in Paléstine at this time. The great powers became deeply embroiled in the affairs of the government in Constantinople and made considerable political and economic inroads in the provinces. Economic links with Europe grew, particularly after the inauguration in the mid-nineteenth century of regular steamship services to the eastern Mediterranean. Through the Capitulations, which gave foreigners immunity from Ottoman law in its domains (trials were conducted under the laws of the nationality concerned), European businessmen and consuls had extraordinary latitude to pursue their interests. In Palestine, the expansion of European trade and commercial intervention was marked but not as extensive as it was in Egypt, Lebanon and Syria.

What particularly characterised European intervention in Palestine was first the question of protection of the Christian holy places, which became a symbolic way for especially France, Russia and Britain to fight for influence – both with each other and with the Turks. Local client communities also became embroiled. The second factor was the development, from the 1880s, of an increasingly systematic colonisation drive by Jewish groups associated with the Zionist movement in Europe.

When the British marched into Palestine from Egypt in 1917, pushing the defeated Turks before them, they already had clear motives for remaining there. These were chiefly strategic. If the French and British were allies in Europe, in the Middle East they were rivals, each intent on carving up an empire to their own best advantage. In a secret agreement made in 1916, the British and French (with Russian acquiescence) delineated the main outlines of the areas to be under their respective control or 'sphere of influence'. In this scheme, Palestine was to be under some form of international control. However, the Bolshevik Revolution and the British military successes of 1917 which left them in control of Jerusalem overtook this concept. If an international administration was ruled out, and independence not seriously considered, the only alternatives were British or French rule. The British were certainly not keen to have the French as neighbours to Egypt on the eastern side of the Suez Canal, which was seen as crucial to imperial communications with India. Palestine was also potentially a useful base in the eastern Mediterranean.

The Balfour Declaration of 1917 was a wartime afterthought to these considerations, though it reflected some sympathy with Zionist aims among sections of the English ruling élite. Balfour, whose name was given to the declaration he made in a letter to the Zionist leader Chaim Weizman pledging that Britain would establish in Palestine a 'National Home' for the Jewish people, was himself firmly convinced of its importance:

The four great powers are committed to Zionism, and Zionism, be it right or wrong, good or bad, is rooted in age-long tradition, in present needs, in future hopes, of far profounder import than the desire and prejudices of the 700,000 Arabs who now inhabit that ancient land. In my opinion that is right.

(A. J. Balfour, 'Memorandum on Syria, Palestine and Mesopotamia', August 1919. Quoted in C. Sykes, *Crossroads to Israel*, London, 1965, p. 17)

Apart, however, from the few who were convinced of the historic destiny of Zionism, most British officials who did not actually have strong doubts about its usefulness considered that, on analogy with their view of white settlers in colonial territories, the new Zionist settlers would 'uplift' the local populace economically with their capital and culturally by their dynamism. What they did not perceive until much later was that Zionism was a nationalist movement which by its very nature had separatist aims. Its undoubted 'dynamism' was inwardly directed to building up the National Home acquired under British protection and the fruits of these efforts were to be dedicated to its furtherance, not to be shared with the local population.

Control over Palestine was conferred on Britain in the form of a mandate – a kind of tutelage for former territories of powers defeated in World War I, which did not, in international law, confer sovereignty on the mandatory power. The newly formed League of Nations was supposed to supervise the mandatory's administration of the territory. In fact, mandates resembled colonial rule in many respects, especially where, as in the British Mandate in Palestine and the French in Syria, colonial servants actually ran the government. League

"BRITISH OFFICIAL COPYRIGHT PHOTOGRAPH"

TURKISH PRISONERS MARCHING THROUGH NABLUS,
PALESTINE   H 14

The Nablus populace looks on as power changes hands: Turkish prisoners of war march through the town as the British take over during 1918.

of Nations control over what they did was negligible. In the Palestine case, there was the added feature that the special status of the Jewish National Home and its inhabitants was written into the Mandate's clauses. There was a High Commissioner who, with his staff, a civil service and a police force manned in their upper echelons by Englishmen, ran the country.

Due to political disagreements about its composition, no legislative council was ever formed. Such power centres as existed outside British authority were located within the confessional framework. The only one with really effective organisational power even within its own community was the Jewish Agency whose position was legitimised by Article 4 of the Mandate:

> An appropriate Jewish agency shall be recognised as a public body for the purpose of advising and cooperating with the Administration of Palestine in such economic, social and other matters as may affect the establishment of the Jewish national home and the interests of the Jewish population in Palestine, and, subject always to the control of the Administration, to assist and take part in the development of the country.

> The Zionist Organization, so long as its organization and constitution are in the opinion of the Mandatory appropriate, shall be recognized as such agency. It shall take steps in consultation with His Britannic Majesty's Government to secure the cooperation of all Jews who are willing to assist in the establishment of the Jewish national home.

The Palestinian Arab* population, by contrast, had no formal structure for dealing with the administration. Bodies like the Supreme Muslim Council, the highest Muslim religious authority in the country, came to perform a mediating role but of course could not formally represent confessional groups other than Muslims. Primarily, this was the result of the structure of the Mandate, which reserved for the Jewish community a special status among the inhabitants. However, another factor was the power structure which had existed under

*The terms 'Palestinian' and 'Arab' will be used, for convenience, interchangeably. Both refer to the Arabic-speaking inhabitants of Palestine, unless otherwise specified.

23

the Ottomans. This had worked on a divide-and-rule principle, splitting confessional groups through the *millet* system and also playing on rivalries between influential families. Power, or access to power, was therefore fragmented. Individual seeking of favours by the influential from the powerful was the norm. This made cohesion and organisation under the British even harder to achieve, especially as they were not unwilling to perpetuate all these divisions.

Palestine resembled a British colony in several respects. There were few natural resources to covet but the British were willing, as the Mandate stipulated, to grant Zionist agencies or private companies assisting them concessions to develop what there was – most importantly water power and potash. Their main concern was that Palestine should remain strategically useful at low cost. Any whisper of deficit financing was frowned on by the Colonial Office and unspent budgetary surpluses were applauded.

Taxation was not as arbitrary a burden on the population as it had been under the Ottomans. It was regularised and collected by British officials but until the mid-1930s the basis of the main tax on agricultural production remained the same – 10-12% of the gross yield of the land, which was widely thought to be inequitable as it taxed costs of production, the same whether the harvest was good or bad, instead of net production. Indirect taxes through collection of customs dues also became heavier in the course of the Mandate and as the economy as a whole and domestic consumers depended more and more on imported goods, this raised the cost of living, particularly in the urban areas.

Attitudes to spending on health, education and other social services were similar to those in other British colonies. They had relatively low priority and were the first to be cut when the Colonial Office decided to economise. From the mid-1930s, expenditure on internal security made up a high proportion of the budget, but from the British point of view this was necessary – to maintain their own foothold and to keep the National Home afloat.

Within the terms of the Mandate, the administration did something – though the Zionists always argued, not enough – to assist the building up of Jewish industry. This was accomplished in the late 1920s mainly through protective tariffs and the abolition of customs dues on raw materials for industry. As far as industrialisation in the Arab sector was concerned, little was done to promote large-scale development. The British seemed to regard small-scale craft industry (which meantime was in difficulties because of competition from factory products, both local and imported) as an appropriate mainstay for the Arab economy.

This was only one aspect of the administration's general wish to maintain the social and economic status quo in Palestinian society, hoping to keep the basic structure intact but at a more prosperous level. The irony was that the very influences which the British imported with them – the National Home policy and increased dependence of Palestine on the world market economy – worked to undermine those social and economic structures. The second influence was common enough throughout the colonial world but the first had some unique features which distinguish Palestine from other colonial situations.

Zionism was a product of nineteenth-century Europe and the problems Jews experienced there, particularly in Central and Eastern Europe and in Russia. Anti-semitism was assuming a new guise as part of the ideology of various nationalist and pan-national movements, bringing a renewed wave of persecution and pogroms late in the century.

One solution resorted to by many Jews was emigration to the United States but the Zionist movement, which emerged at around the same time, argued that the only viable kind of emigration would be to a state or home which would be Jewish. They argued, against the assimilationists, that Jews would only be safe when they had a physical base from which to control their own destiny. Although various other geographical alternatives – including East Africa – were considered, the area most frequently canvassed was Palestine. Although Zionism was for the most part a secular movement, the concept of Palestine as the historical/biblical Jewish homeland has always been a strong element in its ideology.

Some Jews decided to emigrate to Palestine during the Ottoman period with a minimum of organised support. Their success was limited and their reception by the authorities and the local population was to say the least equivocal. It was difficult for such a settler group to establish itself without a strong organisational and financial basis and, more

22

General Sir Edmund Allenby (left) and other Egyptian Expeditionary Force (EEF) commanders after the capture of Jerusalem by the Britisdh. They are shown surveying the city from the vantage point of the German hospice on the Mount of Olives. According to Bishop MacInnes, Anglican Bishop of Jersualem (second from left), the poses were very much for the benefit of the photographer. "We had just been taken all facing the camera, and then the photographer said, before taking the next, – 'Perhaps one or two of you will look in other directions' '' After some joking the Bishop said: " 'Won't Chetwode [General Sir Philip Chetwode] point at something and we'll all look'. So he struck an attitude at once, and everybody turned their heads, and the kodak was snapped. It really comes out very well, and you wouldn't know that everyone was laughing at the moment.'' (From a letter to the Bishop's son quoted with the kind permission of the Jerusalem and East Mission).

important, without a powerful protector. In the age of colonial expansion, the major imperial powers were obvious candidates as protectors. At the time of World War I there was an obvious coincidence between the interests of Britain as an imperial power and Zionism as a settler movement. Both, for different reasons, wanted to be in Palestine.

Although the settlers initially appeared to accept the very vague 'National Home' concept as a way of gaining a foothold in Palestine, private, if not public, statements by Zionist leaders from World War I onwards make it clear that in the long run a Jewish state or at least an independent entity with a Jewish majority was their goal. The key to achieving this was a high level of immigration. Their main bone of contention with Britain and the focus of Palestinian opposition to Zionist settlement was the numbers of Jewish immigrants to be admitted. The other major targets were control over land and natural resources. The former, as we shall see, could not but affect the existing population.

In other respects, the Zionists differed from other white settlers in their approach to colonisation. Separatism was the key to their thinking. This applied to all political strands within the movement, including most of the socialists. Separatism from Palestinians was particularly expressed by the wish to avoid using Arab labour in Jewish enterprises. This was known as the principle of *avoda ivrit* – Hebrew labour. This concept contrasted sharply with the underlying idea of the exploitation of cheap indigenous labour in, for instance, Britain's African settler colonies.

Accompanying the idea of Hebrew labour, however, was a general attitude to the existing population not unfamiliar among Europeans at that time. Unless the indigenous people could be 'useful' they were regarded either as a nuisance or as scarcely worthy of notice. Zionists, deeply involved in their own ideology and its expression in the National Home, often appeared to take the latter view. Those who felt that the Palestinians could not be ignored or left to the British to take care of fell into several categories. One approach, which met with limited practical success, was that Arabs were scheming, power-hungry and venal and therefore could be bribed into acceptance of the National Home. Another more radical solution was to suggest that Palestinians should be removed from the area of historical Palestine and deposited

bag and baggage on the other side of the Jordan. Both these expedients have their supporters to this day. A third view, which then and now commands little support among Zionists, was that co-existence with the Palestinians should be among the movement's foremost preoccupations rather than a tiresome side issue. Jewish indifference turned to hostility once violent resistance by Palestinians became more systematic and led to the build-up of well organised armed strength on the Zionist side. By the end of World War II the Haganah (Jewish Defence Force) was thought to total 48,500. This included 2,000 fulltime soldiers in the Palmach, 4,500 in the Field Corps, 300,000 in the guards and 12,000 in youth groups; the last three groups were part time.

The development of a large-scale Zionist paramilitary force also spelt the parting of the ways with the British, whose main role, in Zionist eyes, was to defend the Jewish community while allowing it breathing space to build up its numbers and economic strength. The fact that the Zionists did not rely on British official funding except in major public works projects which were to their benefit meant the gradual creation of a 'state within a state'. Funding from supporters overseas was substantial and many new immigrants also brought capital with them. Much of this was channelled through various centralised organisations under the overall control of the Jewish Agency into planned development. This high level of organisation and cohesion overrode, in the final analysis, a strong tendency to factional strife. The need to make Zionism successful also appeared increasingly urgent with the growth of Fascist persecution of the Jews in Europe in the 1930s.

Palestinian nationalism, by contrast, growing out of an established social and economic environment rather than an organised colonising or 'pioneering' effort, as Zionism often portrayed itself, had much less basis for organisational cohesion.

The establishment of British rule and of the National Home principle occurred without any consultation with even the established élites in Palestinian society, let alone the population at large. As far as the British were concerned, this was not unusual – non-European peoples at this time were not normally given any say in who ruled them. However in this case, as in Syria under the French, British rule dashed earlier hopes of independence, ill-founded as they may seem with the benefit of hindsight, which had built up from the beginning of World War I. In some respects, the British themselves had encouraged these hopes by using the rhetoric of nationalism to rouse Arab support against the Turks during the war. The spuriousness of this propaganda was confirmed by the rapid demise in 1920 of the 'independent' Arab state under Sharif Faisal, when the French occupied Damascus and threw him out. Many hopes had, nonetheless, been pinned on this short-lived entity as an expression of the pan-Arab ideal held by many Arab nationalists then and since.

Arab nationalism under the Ottomans began with a literary revival which placed most emphasis on the unity of the Arabs' linguistic and cultural heritage. It grew into a political movement mainly among the intelligentsia of Greater Syria which wanted the Arab provinces to be, to one degree or another, independent of Turkish authority. Demands ranged from decentralisation within the Empire to complete independence. All parts of this spectrum of opinion gained in strength after the 1908 Young Turk revolution which rapidly turned to promoting specifically Turkish nationalism and suppressed signs of linguistic, cultural or political independence among its remaining subjects.

After World War I the division of the Middle East into a number of distinct territorial units narrowed the focus of the nationalist movement to concentrate on opposition to their new rulers, British or French. Colonial boundaries, creating new political realities, also created a new focus for national feeling. Pan-Arab sentiments remained, but in the background. In Palestine opposition to Zionist colonisation was the first focus – this later shifted to the British as it became clear that they were determined to maintain the National Home policy as laid down in the Mandate.

Regional and local loyalties, which had also been strong during Ottoman times, coalesced within these new boundaries. A movement which had begun mostly within the urban intelligentsia became more widely diffused in different social strata. In Palestine, hostility to and fear of the effects of Zionist colonisation was in some respects a unifying force.

At the same time, however, repeated evidence of the relative powerlessness of the Palestinians to change the situation resulted in spasms of demoralisation and disorganisation. This stemmed mainly from the Palestinians' relatively limited leverage with the British authorities and their dependence on the services provided by the Mandate government which was far greater than that of the Zionists. It rapidly became clear that only violence made the British sit up and take notice, though even this did not produce any fundamental policy changes.

The other factor which often inhibited coherent political strategies and organisation was the internal divisions in Palestinian society. European observers have usually concentrated on divisions along religious and clan lines, treated as 'given' features of the society, with little acknowledgement that successive governments also contributed to the perpetuation of these forms of identity.

The Turkish *millet* system not only strengthened communal identities but reinforced the political importance of religious ties and the mediating role of religious leaders in politics. The British also tended to accept this classification by religion but the transformation of the Jewish community by the advent of organised Zionism and the National Home policy in fact proved to be a unifying factor for the Arabic-speaking communities, whether Muslim or Christian. Rivalries still existed, particularly in the commercial and employment spheres, but they did not, overall, play a crucial role in shaping the Palestinian nationalist movement. One reversal of privilege did occur, however. In the Ottoman period the majority Muslim community had most access to political power and government appointments. During the Mandate, the Christian community was often favoured, particularly in regard to employment.

Family and clan (groups of extended families claiming the same ancestry) were probably a more potent source of division and as such have been exploited by each ruling power in turn. That these loyalties were frequently linked to a local identity – a region, town or village – added to their strength. Apart from the way in which the authorities played families and clans off against each other, thus reinforcing these loyalties in each generation, some observers argue that family ties of all kinds have been strengthened since 1948 by the insecurities of a stateless existence. Even prior to that, the lack of alternative forms of association and power may have slowed the loosening of those bonds which increased mobility and education might otherwise have caused.

Such forms of identity and power may have been the ones most visible to the outside observer, but they were not the only ones. The power and status which families or clans possessed had an economic base and that base was most commonly the ownership of land. Economically defined class divisions developed to fit European societies of the nineteenth and twentieth centuries can be misleading when applied to societies with different economic and political histories, but this does not alter the fact that class divisions based on economic factors did exist. Control of land and the product of the land was the most important form of wealth in Palestinian society in the nineteenth century. Income came mostly from rents in kind from tenants and sharecroppers, and the proceeds – in the form of agricultural produce – were sold locally or exported. On the whole land was not viewed among established landowning families as a commercial asset to be bought and sold. It was part of their claim to notability and status in the community and was passed on to their children to maintain that position.

By the end of the century, however, another view of land – as a capital asset with a particular exchange value – was becoming more common. Ottoman land law, a tangled and complex affair whose relics have caused confusion in the legal status of cultivators to this day, essentially viewed all agricultural land as, in the final resort, the property of the state (known as *miri* land). Tenure rights depended on constant cultivation. Land which was not cultivated for three consecutive years 'without lawful excuse' reverted to the state and could only be redeemed by payment of its capital value. Attempts to change the land law in order to give individuals secure title to land so that they could sell it or mortgage it as private property failed to achieve the desired results. *De facto*, however, land was changing hands as if it was private property even before World War I.

Demand for land on the commercial market came from several sources – from Jewish and other European colonists; absentee landowners (often non-Palestinian landowners); bankers or merchants making an investment in land; and local merchants, some of whom wanted to cash in on the development of the export market for citrus produce. The latter group clearly had a different attitude to both the land and the tenants or sharecroppers who lived on it and worked it from the older category of landowning families who had local social roots and whose political position depended very much on maintaining patronage relationships with the villages they controlled. Nonetheless, by World War I the younger generation of many of these provincial families began to move to the larger towns, to receive higher education and in some cases to become urban professionals – doctors, teachers, lawyers and so on. In this respect some of the ties of family and local allegiance began to break down.

The major families of Jerusalem were in some ways exceptions, different from either the urban based merchants or the provincial notables. Their prestige rested not only on both urban and rural land ownership but on access to and influence with the Ottoman authorities (to a much lesser extent with the British) and on their claims to certain religious and civic offices. By the mandate period the most important of these were the position of mayor and that of Grand Mufti – the highest religious office. Competition for these offices – manipulated by the British authorities – and for leadership of the nationalist movement between the two most powerful families in the mandate period – the Hussainis and the Nashashibis – had national repercussions, at times splitting the Palestinian community nationally into two distinct camps.

While there is no doubt that individuals and families among the landowning and merchant classes prospered during the British period, their power as a group was diminished economically and politically. For those whose main interests lay in ownership of agricultural land, there was the option (nationalist scruples aside) to sell it at high prices. Where, however, landownership carried with it political and social status, there was a tendency not to sell up completely.

Reinvestment of capital so realised in industrial enterprise was not a popular option, although the overall direction of the economy was towards industrial development, albeit by slower stages than is often imagined. The risks were high, the competition from Jewish industry considerable and the required technological and managerial know-how was inevitably rare in a class whose wealth had previously rested mostly on non-capitalist agriculture.

By the 1930s and early 1940s, the situation of the peasantry who had been the backbone of the land-

23
*Ragheb Nashashibi reading
the address of welcome to the
first High Commissioner, Sir
Herbert Samuel, in 1920. A
leading member of a powerful
Jerusalem family which
played an important part in
politics throughout the
Mandate, Nashashibi
represented the section of
Palestinian society which,
while rejecting Zionism,
generally wanted to find a*
modus vivendi *with the
British.*

owners' powerbase was slowly changing so that fewer people depended exclusively on landowners' bounty or credit. Even limited access to wage labour and other forms of credit loosened the ties. In the towns too, new forms of organisation emerged which did not depend so directly on the old kinds of patronage.

The social and political tensions created by these old and new allegiances were not resolved by the end of the Mandate. The rebellions of 1936 — 1939 certainly expressed many of the conflicts within the society as well as demonstrating the Palesti- nians' hostility to both British rule and Zionism, but did not produce any clear-cut rearrangement of power relations – either within the society itself or with its rulers. Further evolution of these relation- ships was subsequently cut short by the events of 1947-9 which left the great majority of Palestinians as stateless persons, many of them refugees, and the remainder (less than 200,000) under Israeli rule, marking the beginning of changes in Palestinian society far more drastic than anything which had come before.

PURCHASES OF LAND BY THE THREE MAIN JEWISH LAND COMPANIES – PICA (PALESTINE JEWISH COLONISATION ASSOCIATION), PALESTINE LAND DEVELOPMENT COMPANY AND THE JEWISH NATIONAL FUND – UP TO 1936

	Dunums*	Percentage
Acquired from large absentee landowners	358,974	52.6
Acquired from large resident landowners	167,802	24.6
Acquired from Government, Churches and foreign companies	91,001	13.4
Acquired from fellaheen (farmers)	64,201	9.4
	681,978	

(A. Granott, *The Land System in Palestine*, London, 1952, p. 278)

AREAS PURCHASED BY JEWS, 1920-1945

Year	Dunums★
Area owned before 1920 (estimated)	650,000
1920	1,048
1921	90,785
1922	39,359
1923	17,493
1924	44,765
1925	176,124
1926	38,978
1927	18,995
1928	21,515
1929	64,517
1930	19,365
1931	18,585
1932	18,893
1933	36,991
1934	62,114
1935	72,905
1936	18,146
1937	29,367
1938	27,280
1939	27,973
1940	22,481
1941	14,530
1942	18,180
1943	18,035
1944	8,311
1945 (estimate)	11,000
Total	1,588,365

(*Survey of Palestine 1945-46*, Vol I, p. 244)

★Note: one acre = approximately four dunums.

Plains

Uninhabited Hill, Wilderness

Desert

Beersheba Area

Inhabited Hills

Water.

International Boundaries

Primary Roads

Main geographical features

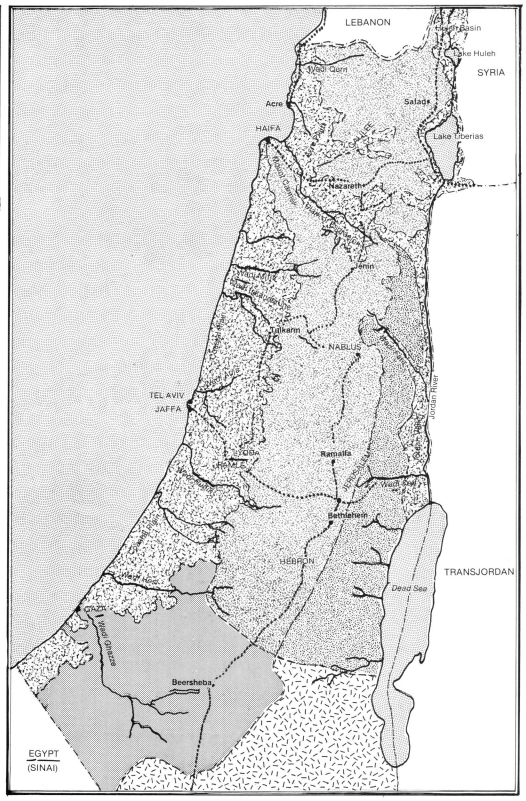

LEBANON

Huleh Basin

Lake Huleh

SYRIA

Wadi Qurn

Acre

Safad

HAIFA

Lake Tiberias

GALILEE

Mount Carmel

Nazareth

Jenin

Wadi Milh

Wadi Iskanderune

Tulkarm

NABLUS

Wadi Arfa

TEL AVIV

JAFFA

Jordan River

LYDDA

RAMLE

Ramalla

JERUSALEM

Wadi Sun

Bethlehem

Wadi Kdt

HEBRON

TRANSJORDAN

Dead Sea

Wadi Hesi

GAZA

Wadi Ghazze

Beersheba

EGYPT
(SINAI)

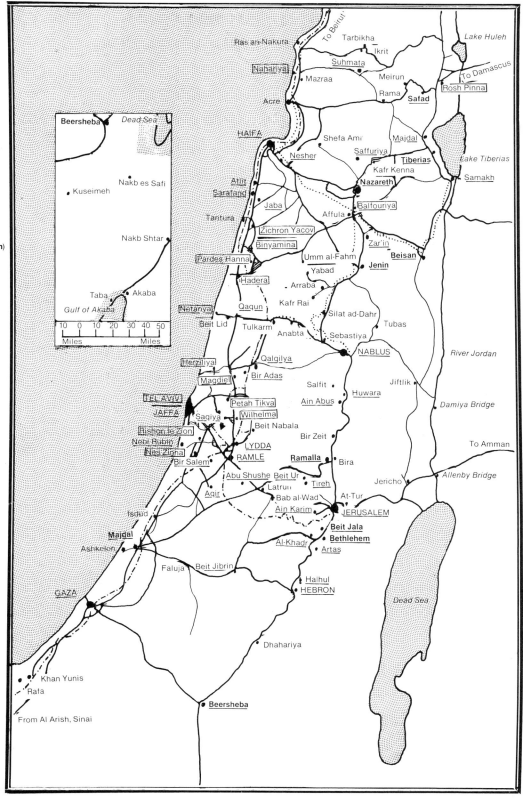

1

'Boy with sling'. While slings certainly were used by children, David and Goliath were clearly not far from photographer Matson's mind.

2

'An Arab cultivator and his prehistoric plough . . . husbandry is conducted today just as it was in the days of the Old Testament' reads the caption by Owen Tweedy, Middle East correspondent of the Daily Telegraph *from 1927 to 1930. In contrast to many other observers who wrote in a similar vein, however, he does go on to say that these methods of husbandry were actually quite appropriate to the terrain.*

1 LAND AND VILLAGE LIFE

Land was the prime source of wealth and livelihood in Palestinian society. Until the end of the Mandate some 60% of the population (excluding Jews) depended on agriculture and related occupations for their living. For a smaller number of people, land, agricultural and urban, was their source of wealth, though through ownership rather than labour. Attachment to the land was for most people therefore not a sentimental notion but a matter of practical necessity, though subsequent loss has now made such tenacious attachment appear romanticised. Nonetheless, as many who feel this attachment would probably admit, peasant live was hardly paradise. It did however provide not only a livelihood but a focus of identity common in peasant societies, based on ties of kinship and identification with village or district.

It is this last aspect which is very hard to discern from photographs. Pictures of rural communities were almost always taken by foreigners, government officials or townspeople. The tourists sought the picturesque, or in the Palestinian case, scenes they considered 'biblical'. It is also noteworthy that this type of picture is seldom given a geographical location which, in a country where local differences were important, is also a form of distortion. The government official, during the Mandate period, usually perceived and photographed villagers as 'problems' of one sort or another – dirty, poor, ignorant and backward – all faults he was supposed (usually on a rather low budget) to rectify.

3

'The neglected future generation'. Children in the village of Saffuriya, near Nazareth, as seen by a Palestinian employee of the British-run education department (early 1930s).

35

4

Mud houses in the village of Zar'in (sometimes called by the biblical name of Jezreel) on the southern edge of the Esdraelon valley. The inhabitants were mostly migrants from the hill country mixed with bedouin who had settled to agriculture. By the end of the Ottoman period, the bulk of the village lands were owned by one of the district's major landowning families, the Abdul Hadis.

Villages

The physical character of villages varied according to the terrain. Locally available materials were employed for building – stone in the hills, mud, clay and straw on the plains. Wood was sparingly used as it was in scarce supply in most areas. The hill villages give an impression of greater permanence partly owing to the solidity of stone buildings, but also because most of them had longer histories of continuous occupation than those on the plains.

In the early nineteenth century there were few villages on the coastal plain and in the valley of Esdraelon, because the bedouin at that time occupied these areas in strength and, in any event, much of the coastal plain was malarial. By the 1880s, however, Laurence Oliphant was describing the valley of Esdraelon as resembling 'a huge green lake of waving wheat' and the cultivated area on the coast was also being extended. This was not just due to the efforts of Jewish and German Protestant colonists who were beginning to establish themselves there but also because villagers from the western slopes of the hills were starting to cultivate land in the plains below. At first they would simply go down to plant and to harvest their crops. Gradually some of the temporary shelters they used while working there were developed into mud houses and small subsidiary villages called *khirba*s grew up. Some of these *khirba*s eventually became quite large settlements.

5

Huwara, a stone-built village in the hills south of Nablus, with a population of 1,300 in 1944. This was a settlement of long standing; the Survey of Western Palestine *commented in 1881 that 'it has an appearance of antiquity'.*

During World War I, when the coastal plain was affected by fighting, cultivation became difficult or impossible and most of the inhabitants of these *khirba*s retreated to the parent villages in the hills. After the war, they were redeveloped, particularly along the edge of the hills from the valley of Esdraelon south towards Ramle. The establishment of the border in 1948 between the State of Israel and what has since been known as the West Bank cut off some of these villages from their land and *khirba*s in the plains.

6

Building a stone house in a village in the hill country. The construction of the roof was a festive occasion in which all the neighbours joined, with women as well as men helping to carry stone and mortar and passing it up to the workers on the roof, under the supervision of the head mason. At the feast to celebrate the completion of the house, he would receive a present – usually a coat or robe.

7

Aerial photo of an area south of Nablus (see map). The village to the right is Huwara, seen at ground level on the previous page. Its total land area was 7,982 dunums (one acre = approximately four dunums) of which 5,465 dunums were cultivated – 4,858 dunums with field crops and 607 dunums with orchards and irrigated crops. To the left is Ain Abus, a much smaller village with a population of 340 and a total land area of 4,011 dunums, of which 2,107 were planted with field crops and 539 were orchards and irrigated land. There was a spring to the west of the village, which may have watered olive groves in the valley just behind the village and the gardens surrounding it. Another olive grove can be seen on the hillslope south of the road. In both villages a substantial amount of land is uncultivated, because the soil on some of the hillsides was poor and the ground rocky. Animals might be grazed on this rough land.

Patterns of Land Tenure

These aerial photographs were taken in 1944 by the Royal Air Force. The first photograph shows a fertile stretch of land in the hill country just south of Nablus. Almost all the land in the valley is cultivated – mostly with field crops, typically wheat, sesame and durra (sorghum). Some land might also be used for vegetables which were becoming important as a cash crop in the later years of the Mandate. Surrounding the villages are gardens where fruit trees and vegetables were commonly grown. On the hill slopes, which were terraced to prevent erosion, trees were mostly grown. The most important tree crop in this region was olives, the oil from which was the main ingredient in the local Nablus soap-making industry. Sometimes soap manufacturers or merchants would purchase a whole year's crop in advance from a village or individual owner in order to ensure their supplies.

The photographs were taken in December just around the time of planting winter field crops; the newly ploughed areas can be seen quite clearly. Some land was usually left fallow every year to prevent exhaustion of the soil, but chemical fertilisers were not widely used.

It is unfortunate that there is not a comparable picture for the early 1930s, as this might show some interesting contrasts. The early 1940s were a particularly good time for the agricultural sector. Controls on imports and growth of local demand raised prices, particularly on commodities like wheat and olive oil. It is likely that more land was being cultivated in this area in 1944 than would have been the case in the early 1930s when prices were very low and the hill areas had a series of disastrous seasons.

8

Terracing on hillsides was vital to prevent soil erosion. To this day, one way of judging the prosperity of an area is by the condition of the terracing, which required an extra investment of time and labour, both for upkeep and for the opening up of new land.

39

The second photograph was taken some way to the west of the first. The aircraft flew along the line of a valley which comes out on the coastal plain near Qalqilya. This picture is of the area just west of Qalqilya and shows the contrast between a Jewish settlement (Magdiel) and a small Arab village (Bir Adas). Most Jewish settlements were in the plains where large-scale irrigated agriculture was easier to achieve and communications were reasonably good. Although the village and the settlement both grew citrus crops, the difference in both layout of housing and patterns of land tenure is striking. The village is patterned typically for a Palestinian rural community with the houses bunched close together, gardens around it and roads or paths radiating into the orange groves and fields. Some Jewish settlements were arranged in a similarly defensible fashion with roads radiating out from a central cluster of houses, but Magdiel was a *moshav* (co-operative village) in which land was owned individually and houses are dotted along the roads in proximity to their plots.

Landownership in the village was more complex. The crop pattern was less specialised (half citrus, half field crops) and land owned by one family or individual could be scattered in different parts of the village. This resulted from a system of collective village tenure prevalent until some ten or fifteen years before this picture was taken. The arrangement, called *mushaa*, allocated each head of family a series of plots of land which would represent a reasonably fair share of the various qualities of land available. Before this century it was customary to rotate these shares every five or six years.

Collective tenure by villages had been virtually abolished in the plains by the 1940s but in many places peasants still owned a number of separate plots scattered around the village. This pattern of ownership applied sometimes to land in the hill valleys but seldom to tree-planted hillsides. These were mostly in individual tenure. However where there was *mushaa* tenure in the hills it was abolished later than in the plains. Pressure to hold individual title to land so that it could be readily bought and sold was greatest on the plains. Land certainly changed hands in the hill districts but on nothing like the scale that occurred along the coast and in Esdraelon valley. The only exception by the 1940s was Galilee where the Zionists were beginning to buy up land for reasons which owed more to strategic than strictly agricultural considerations.

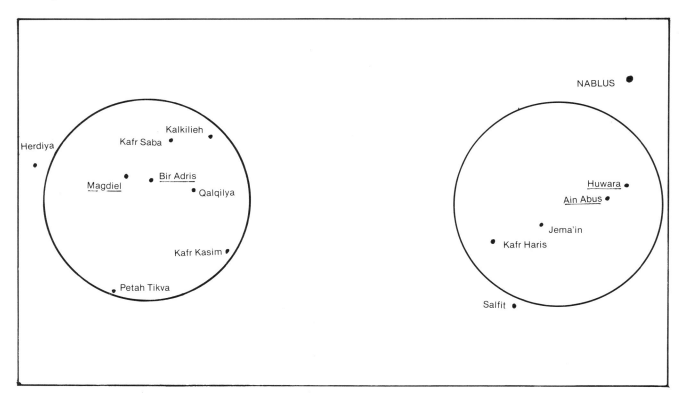

9

To the right is the Arab village of Bir Adas, which in 1944 had a population of 300 and a land area of 5,492 dunums of which 1,604 dunums were planted with citrus and bananas (bananas are the very dark patches in the photograph) while much of the remainder was devoted to cereal crops. A small amount of village land (109 dunums) was Jewish-owned. To the left is the Jewish settlement moshav Magdiel, established in 1924, with a population of 1,260 in 1944. The total land area was 3,660 dunums of which 2,533 dunums were devoted to citrus and bananas. In both these settlements, Jewish and Arab, the proportion of cultivated to total land area is much higher than in the hills. Bir Adas was destroyed after 1948.

41

Working the Land

10

'Woman at the well', a favourite subject for photographers in search of New Testament themes. Here a carefully posed shot is perhaps suggestive of the Samaritan woman at the well. In fact, the town in the background is Bethlehem. The woman's bared arms seem an unusual feature, but in fact dresses worn by women in this area had wide, pointed sleeves which were often tied up out of the way while working. Carrying water from the nearest well or spring was a daily task, normally performed by women and children.

The sort of pictures Europeans took of Palestinian rural life frequently emphasise the unchanging nature of cultivation. This idea focused almost exclusively on the technology of agriculture and rested on the assumption, perhaps inevitable in the confident atmosphere of early twentieth-century western Europe and the United States, that if technology does not change, all else stands still. A simple wooden plough or threshing board 'as used in biblical times' symbolised backwardness, quaint and picturesque though it might be.

Aside from the possibility of arguing that this kind of plough was actually quite well suited to the soil and terrain on which it was used, the preoccupations of this kind of photography did not allow it to be put in a context which might explain why the technology had not changed. This was frequently ascribed to ignorance or, less charitably, stupidity, but seldom to the fact that most peasants could not afford any equipment which could not be made in the village and then mostly with locally available materials. Indebtedness was very common and certainly few smallholders had any capital to make expensive technical improvements. This of course bred a cautious and conservative attitude

11

Children from the village of Suhmata in Acre subdistrict carrying water in pottery jars and a kerosene can which at the time (1932) was becoming a popular container with all kinds of uses. Water for domestic use was scarce and up to the end of the Mandate most villages did not have piped water, so all supplies had to be carried in this way. In the hills, most villages which had a nearby water source used it to irrigate the gardens and orchards around the houses.

to new methods as their failure could prove economically disastrous. Technical innovation did occur on a small scale but, much more importantly, the wider economic context in which peasant agriculture functioned was slowly but decisively altered, though its technology remained much the same.

Probably the most important technical constraint on increased productivity and new farming methods was lack of water. This was equally true of other parts of the Middle East where rainfall was only just sufficient to secure a rather precarious living from agriculture. Annual average figures are also rather deceptive as rainfall in this region fluctuates a great deal from year to year.

12

13

12 13

In the plains, irrigation became more common during the mandate, mostly on large-scale citrus plantations. Above a water wheel in the southern plains near Ashkelon. A camel turns the wheel which raises the chain of buckets from the well.

An iron girder has been substituted here for the original wooden beam holding up the wheel. Another way of raising water from a deep well was by using a yoke of oxen, as below.

14

15

14 15

Animals were commonly used as a means of propulsion – as here, in oil presses and in flour mills. They therefore had not simply a commercial value – to be bought and sold for their meat and milk – but were a vital element in agricultural life. Most families who were not desperately poor kept some animals for ploughing and reared sheep, goats and poultry to provide for their own needs. Very often children were given the job of looking after these animals. The misty timelessness of these 'shepherd' photographs is broken in one detail – in the top picture the child with its back to the camera holds what looks like a commercially bottled drink.

16 *This photograph comes from a luridly tinted glass slide labelled 'the Good Shepherd', ready to defend himself and his sheep with a rather antiquated rifle. Ironically, given the biblical connotations of being a shepherd in Palestine, it was not a particularly high status job. Professional shepherds were said to be increasingly hard to find by the 1930s. The following 'job description' comes from data collected by the Ramalla Farmers' Association in 1922:*

1. *Function*	*Pasturing and guarding sheep, goats and cattle.*
2. *Employers*	*Owners of large herds and flocks or several small owners by combination.*
3. *Wages*	*£E.10-15 a year, plus food and clothes, or P.T.2-3 per sheep or goat per month. P.T.10-15 per cow per month.*
4. *Contract*	*Monthly or yearly, or per head.*
5. *Places of Supply*	*From village or adjacent villages.*
6. *Total employed*	*200-300 (mostly to the Eastern side of the Sub-District).*
7. *Hours of work*	*Summer, 6 a.m. to 6 p.m. (two hours midday rest for watering). Winter, 8 a.m. to 4 p.m.*

16

The wages given by this survey for this and other jobs may be higher than average for the Mandate period as the immediate post-war period up to 1923 saw inflation of prices and wages which subsequently dropped away.
Note:
The money values here are denominated in Egyptian pounds and piastres (P.T. 100 = £E1) – the official currency from World War I until 1927 when it was replaced by the Palestine pound (1000 mils = £P1).
(£P1 = £1 sterling; £E1 = £0.975 sterling)

17

Sheep-shearing. Sheep and goats provided meat, milk, wool, skins, cheese and leben (yoghurt). Goat's hair was also used for making sacks and by the bedouin for making their tents. Although commercial sales of meat and cheese by peasant farmers were comparatively rare, during the Mandate the expanding demand for meat in the urban areas (Palestine became a large importer of meat) led some richer merchants and farmers to breed herds strictly for commercial purposes and hire shepherds to tend them.

17

18
A beautiful study which has some odd features. First, it is labelled 'Arab string-maker' – in fact it is a man spinning wool. Second, another glass slide version of the same picture shows the same man performing the same action, but with his sheepskin coat turned skin side out – the more usual way to wear it.

19
A less technically beautiful and more unpretentious photograph of the same 'drop and spin' method. It was easy and portable, consisting simply of dropping and spinning around two crossed sticks to which the yarn was attached and playing out the wool through the fingers.

47

20

A 'curiosity' photograph of an unequal plough team. It is also another illustration of how ownership of suitable animals was one measure of wealth – to own a good ploughing team of oxen was a great advantage. The death of animals through disease or drought – which happened quite often – could easily lead to this seemingly bizarre situation if no more suitable combination was available. The only other alternative, which many peasants could not afford, would be to hire a ploughman and team.

21

A British Agriculture Department demonstration in the early 1930s of ploughing with a European-manufactured tractor. The picture was taken by a Palestinian agricultural extension officer working in Hebron subdistrict. Tractor ploughing was by this time more common in the plains (to which it was better suited than in the hills) but the capital outlay was beyond all but rich landowners and entrepreneurs and Jewish settlements. Also petrol to run a tractor remained expensive.

22

23

22 23

In many parts of Palestine, it was common for women to share in agricultural work. Ploughing was considered a man's job – there was a quite strict division of labour – while women weeded the fields, planted some of the summer crops and supervised livestock. In the central hill region, some sharecropping arrangements specified that the sharecropper would receive a share of the harvest in return, not just for his own labour for the season, but also that of a female relative.
Below:
an invisible baby hanging in a sling while its mother was working.

49

24

Harvest time – spread from April to September for different crops – was the busiest time of year. The whole family worked in the fields, harvesting, threshing, winnowing and picking fruit and olives.

25
'Reapers' repast'.

26 27 28

Threshing wheat with a flail and with a drag, a kind of sledge with sharp stones inserted in holes on the underside which was pulled (below) by a muzzled team of oxen.

27

26

28

29

Winnowing. The man in the tarbush might be the landowner come to look over the crop — by his dress, he does not 'belong' in the scene.

30

30

Curing sesame. Sesame, unlike wheat, barley and durra was a cash crop which, even in the nineteenth century, was exported as far afield as France.

31

31

Piles of durra (sorghum) on the threshing floor in the village of Qaqun in Tulkarm subdistrict. The threshing floor was usually a flat area near the village where all the crops were gathered. People very often slept out at the floor during threshing to guard their crops. To establish ownership they would impress their pile with their own particular seal. At this stage the crop was divided up into what would have to be sold to pay taxes and debts; another part might be for rent paid in kind; another part might be the quarter or fifth of the crop due to a sharecropper who had worked the season for the farmer.

32 33

Picking olives – a major commercial crop in the hill area. In the nineteenth century olive oil was used for lighting, before it was superceded by imported kerosene, as well as for eating and for soap making.

34
Tree crops became more popular during the Mandate, encouraged by government agriculturalists, one of whom is seen here instructing peasants how to care for seedlings. These trees, however, were a very long-term investment – olive trees take ten years to come to full bearing – and only richer peasants could afford the risks involved.

35
Pruning vines, grown mainly in the area around Jerusalem. Grapes were eaten fresh or preserved as a kind of cheese; wine-making was not common.

37

36 37

Various methods of extracting oil from olives: using a millstone to produce small amounts for home consumption and in a large mill driven by a camel for commercial production.

Domestic work was entirely the woman's domain. Usually the directing force in organising the household would be the wife though, if she were young, her mother-in-law might be in control. Children were expected to help. Most work was done in the courtyard when the weather was good — here women are seen working in the courtyard of a house in the village of Ain Karim, close to Jerusalem (1933).
Below:
cooking a meal over a small clay stove fuelled with brushwood in the village of Artas, south of Jerusalem. The women shown here are servants, signifying that the household is one of the richer ones in the village.

38

39

40

40 41

Domestic work was not just cleaning, cooking and looking after children. Because villagers until the end of the Mandate continued to grow at least a proportion of their own food, there was a good deal of processing to be done.
Above:
a woman sifts wheat for grinding (1933). The photographer could not resist a biblical allusion here. The reference to Luke 22:31 'And the Lord said: Simon, Simon, Satan hath desired to have you, that he may sift you as wheat' is not much help in understanding the photograph.
Below:
a woman grinding wheat between millstones.

41

42

Young women of Abu Shushe village in Ramle subdistrict gathering herbs for cooking.

42

43 44

Since few people had their own oven, bread was baked in the communal village oven. In the second photograph, the woman has drawn her veil over her face, presumably because of the presence of a (male) outsider and his camera. Village women were not usually veiled.

45
Churning butter in a skin bag.

46

*Drying manure for fuel.
Manure and brushwood
substituted for wood, which
was very scarce. Manure was
not used as a fertiliser.*

47

Village Crafts

Village identity remained very strong and well-defined despite a gradual increase in mobility which took people away from their place of birth to work, to study, or occasionally even to emigrate. Women might also move from one village to another when they got married. By and large, however, people did not expect to move far or for very long during their lives. Village and family ties anyway remained of great importance for those who moved away.

One particular craft tradition which vividly expressed this sense of identity was the embroidery of women's dresses. The combination of the design of the dress and the patterns of embroidery on it would show distinctly and precisely not just the social standing of the wearer but the village and region the person came from. Women could thus be identified by village or town at social gatherings, at festivals like Nebi Musa or Nebi Rubin (annual Muslim religious celebrations which attracted people from many parts of the country), and in the market towns to which village women went to buy and sell produce. Men, by contrast, had no such precise markers of identity. Although the most splendid dresses were reserved for feast days, marriage and other important occasions, both embroidered dresses, headdresses decorated with coins and other jewellery were also part of everyday wear.

48

47 48

Embroidery was usually done in groups – often in the afternoons when other domestic chores were finished and women had time to sit together with relatives and neighbours to sew and talk. Appealing though the solitary girl's absorption in her work may be to the viewer, it was probably not typical. The other setting – the Ramalla Women's Union – is unusually formal. The two women in light dresses on the right are wearing characteristic versions of the Ramalla dress – red and black embroidery on cream linen.

49

49 50

*The richly embroidered dress
of the villages around
Jerusalem with the short
jacket and long pointed
sleeves.*
Above:
*the daughter of the village
shaikh of Ain Karim in
festive costume.*
Below:
*a married woman from
Bethlehem wearing the
distinctive tall hat and veil
only found in that town.*

50

The embroidery was not just the preserve of the well-to-do or leisured. It was a common activity for village women, both Muslim and Christian. Mothers taught daughters and handed on the patterns, though intriguing variations were made according to the inventiveness of individuals. Fabrics were usually linen (especially for dresses in the Ramalla area), indigo-dyed cotton (mostly from the town of Majdal in the south where weaving was still an important craft) or silk from Syria. The import of a variety of fabrics from Europe in the 1920s and 1930s introduced some changes, including the use of velvet. European sewing and embroidery threads also took over from local ones.

Not all areas of the country attached the same importance to this decorative tradition. The richest and most prolific dress embroidery was to be found in the Jerusalem area, in the villages from Ramalla south to Bethlehem, Hebron and Beersheba. It was also important in villages on the coastal plain around Jaffa. In Galilee embroidery was more sparing and in the central range of hills around Nablus and Jenin dresses were rarely embroidered although quite elaborate and colourful decoration with silk patches can be seen on dresses from Nablus. The reason for this is not entirely clear, though one part of the explanation may be that in the Nablus area women were generally more involved in agricultural work and so had less time to spare than women in the rather better-off villages who might not have as much labour in the fields to add to their domestic work.

51
Women from Lydda, wearing dresses without embroidery and made partly from European flowered print material.

51

52
Another of those irresistably striking scenes which caught the photographer's eye – peasant women wearing their distinctive local dresses which would identify their origins when they came, as on this occasion, to market their cauliflowers in Jerusalem.

52

53

54

53 54

Women wore embroidered dresses, headdresses and jewellery on ordinary workaday occasions. Here (above) a younger woman crushes clay and an older pair (below) knead the dampened clay to make the hand-thrown pottery which was a women's speciality in the villages. As they broke quite easily, each year a new batch of dishes, pots and bowls would have to be made. Tin cans began to encroach as a substitute in the 1920s and 1930s.

55

PLOUGH REPAIRER

1. Function	Repairing wooden parts of ploughs.
2. Employers	20 to 50 farmers of village.
3. Wages	Paid in kind: 10 to 15 rotl of wheat per plough per season, £E 25 to £50 a season.
4. Contract	Individual contracts to do all repairs required during ploughing season to 20 to 50 ploughs.
5. Places of Supply	Local: 1 or 2 to each village.
6. Total employed	100.
7. Hours of work	Irregular.
8. Season employed	December to April.
9. Output or scope	Repairs to 20 to 50 ploughs a season.
10. Remarks	Repairs to iron parts of plough (share, binding pieces, etc.) have to be taken to nearest blacksmith.

From: Ramalla Farmers' Association

55 56 57

Most agricultural implements in common use could be made and mended locally. This kind of work, like the pottery just shown, was done in the slack agricultural season after the harvest. Here a carpenter mends ploughs, sickles are sharpened and a blacksmith shoes a donkey.

56

57

Social life in villages, except perhaps those close to large towns, changed less than did economic or political circumstances. In some ways, the upheavals going on in the country at large may have made people more inclined to cling to familiar, well-tried lifestyles and social relationships wherever this was possible.

Village relationships – both with family and neighbours – were conducted much more publicly than would be the case in a town. This is a common enough feature of small communities but it was reinforced in this case by the fact that houses, with the exception of a few belonging to the wealthier village *shaikh,* landowner or merchant, were small and cramped. Apart from sleeping and sheltering from the cold or rain, most of life happened out of doors – in courtyards, on doorsteps and in the street. As far as the photographer was concerned, this made village social activities more 'visible' than they would have been in towns.

Births, deaths, marriages, circumcisions, return of a relative or friend from military service or from prison – all these and more were marked by some kind of village celebration or mourning, as the case might be. These would not be confined to the immediate family, though obviously the scope of the festivities would depend on the state of the family's finances. A poor sharecropper could not (without a richer relative) compete with the spread laid on by the village *shaikh* or landowner. Nonetheless these occasions would often tax a family's funds quite heavily and might throw individuals into debt. British administrators and others often fulminated against such 'irrational' and wasteful practices. While they undoubtedly did sometimes result in real hardship, on the whole these village social occasions were a part of a network of relations of mutual obligation, particularly among members of an extended family or clan *(hamula)*. Service and hospitality was provided in the knowledge that the same could be expected in return on another occasion.

The better-off were expected to be generous and meanness was usually treated with contempt. Although village society was by no means egalitarian – there were always discrepancies in wealth and power between individuals, families and clans and these probably on the whole increased rather than decreased over the period –

the very poor and indigent could usually rely on at least some help and support, though this was not without its price.

58

Guest houses were the focus of (male) social life where villagers met and entertained anyone visiting or passing through the village. These often belonged to local notable families – in larger villages or small towns there would be several belonging to different families or clans. To keep a well-provided guest house enhanced the owner's prestige.

Villages often laid claim to a local saint – sometimes a widely famous figure but often a revered local notable. The picture below shows the shrine of Shaikh Jada near Ramle. Sometimes shrines were not buildings but trees of certain kinds or even streams, both of which were considered precious because of their scarcity. Offerings – food, oil or burning candles – were made at shrines in the hope of favours, or in fulfilment of vows. Rags were sometimes tied to trees as offerings. Property left in the vicinity of a shrine – especially agricultural implements or gathered crops – were considered safe from theft because it was universally understood that they were under the saint's protection. While Christian and Muslim villages normally had different saints and shrines, a few were venerated by both – al-Khadr (St George the Green) was a case in point.

Little piles of stones dotted the landscape as in the centre picture. These sometimes marked boundaries between properties but often they were part of a pilgrim's reverence to a nearby saint's shrine passed on the road. Tokens – stones, pottery or buttons – were also left on grave stones, as in the top picture.

60

61

62

62 63

*Two contrasting wedding
processions. The first –
though no indication was
given on the slide of the
location or identities of bride
and groom – is clearly the
marriage of a person of some
substance. The second, near
Majdal in the vicinity of*

*Lake Tiberias, is a more
modest affair without flags
and pomp. The bridal party
also sit in panniers on a
camel, but in this case the
panniers are made out of
precariously balanced packing
cases.*

Village communities had high birth rates and high death rates – the first intended to counteract the second. The national average infant mortality in 1930 was 170 and 134 per thousand for the Muslim and Christian communities respectively, so in villages with poor water supplies, no sanitation and minimal health services, it was probably higher. Families assumed the need to have quite a large number of children to allow for probable deaths. The average size of a nuclear family was between five and eight in the 1930s and 1940s. A gradual fall in the death rate during the Mandate meant that population growth was overall among the highest in the world in the 1930s and 1940s.

In Ottoman times epidemic diseases like cholera and typhus were much dreaded and sometimes brought life almost to a standstill in town and countryside though during the mandate these illnesses were successfully brought under control. Death and illness, as much as birth, then, were common occurrences in any village.

Solitariness in any of these states was unusual and relatives and friends would be present at births and would sit constantly with the sick and dying. Both mourning and celebration were public and demonstrative. Both before and during funerals women would wail and tear their clothes, though judging by (mostly male) comments recorded in a study of the village of Artas (south of Jerusalem) by Hilma Granqvist in the 1930s, these practices did not meet with universal approval.

Birth was usually treated in a matter-of-fact way and no special preparations were made. The pregnant woman would probably have the help of women relatives and of the village midwife. Afterwards, the extent of celebrations depended very much on whether the child was a boy or a girl, the former being favoured.

Women living in village or in bedouin society did not as a rule lead such physically sheltered lives as women in towns since they were expected to work alongside their menfolk in agriculture for at least part of the year. Their personal wishes were, however, subordinated on most occasions to the wishes of their menfolk – their fathers before marriage and their husbands after it. The husband's family, his mother particularly, also were influential in determining how pleasant or otherwise life was for a wife. In case of ill-treatment, however, a retreat to her own family was usually possible as long as they could be made to sympathise with her situation.

63

Marriage was normally a family affair, not a matter of individual choice. Though this was more markedly the case for the woman, potential bridegrooms were not immune from family pressures either. Despite the common notion that child brides were the order of the day, data on the age of marriage computed by the 1931 census produced, for the Muslim community, surprising late average ages at marriage – about 20 for women and 25 for men. Even allowing for inevitable inaccuracies and misreporting of ages – deliberate or otherwise – these figures do not reinforce the impression that marriage at 14 or 15 for women was the norm. Early betrothal, however, was more common. It was possible for parents to betroth their offspring at the cradleside, but while this may have strengthened the bonds between two families at the time it did not always finally lead to marriage.

64

*Sword dance at a wedding
accompanied by drums and
flute.*

65

*Bridegroom being led to his
wedding on horseback,
probably in the Ramalla
area.*

Older married women in general had more status in the community and a widow, at least in theory, could not be forced by her family to marry against her will. Although she was permitted to control property, she would usually at least seek the aid and support of her father, brother or other male relatives in doing so.

Dowries (which in the mandate period seemed to range from £P 25 to £P 150) were paid initially to the bride's father, in part as compensation for the loss of her labour to his household. The dowry could be paid in money or sometimes in land or other goods. The father would then give a portion of it to the bride, usually in the form of jewellery. The coin headdresses seen around the Jerusalem area were often part of this. The coins were of some value, sometimes foreign coins like Maria Teresa dollars or the Turkish *beshlik*. In very difficult times women would sell coins from their caps, but this was done with great reluctance as they would usually prefer to pass the headdresses on to their daughters.

The actual style of marriage celebrations varied between Muslim and Christian villages and from area to area. As a rule, however, there were a number of different celebrations marking each stage of proceedings – the engagement, the bridegroom's purchase of the bride's dress, and the festivities occurring in the two or three days around the actual ceremony.

66

Another cause of celebrations – when a son completed reading the Koran for the first time. This was the main content of education provided in old-style village schools (kuttub) run usually by the local religious shaikh. (see also p.75). This picture was taken in the village of Jabba on Mount Carmel. The son standing to the left of the father, whom the photographer has decapitated, had just completed his reading and the village gave a party for him. The father was working as a cook at a nearby British archaeological dig and the photograph was taken by one of the members of the dig.

67

Children in Ain Karim dancing on the roof of their house during the Nebi Musa festival (see p. 139).

1
*High Commissioner Sir
Harold MacMichael meeting
village leaders. The exact
date and place are not known,
but the photograph was taken
by D. G. MacGillivray, a
colonial service official who
acted as Sir Harold's private
secretary from 1938-42. By
this period, relations between
British officials and villagers
had been severely strained by
three years of rebellion and
violence.*

2 VILLAGES AND THE WIDER WORLD

Even in the 1930s and 1940s villages often appeared – to the observer and probably to the inhabitants as well – quite isolated and immune from pressures in the world outside. In practice this had never been entirely true and was certainly not so by that time. The impact of local political events was sufficient to cause villagers to take to the hills in rebellion, and economic and political events in the outside world had become more and more important in determining whether a village prospered or struggled. The increased need to find money to pay taxes, rents and other costs had pushed more peasants to produce at least some marketable cash crops. At the same time, Palestine's small marketplace was not isolated from currents on the world's commodity markets, and the apparently improbable connections which might link the US grain market and the supposedly biblical Palestinian peasant became more and more of a reality.

Governments and Peasants

In Ottoman times, government intervention in village life, except where the collection of taxes was concerned, was minimal. Local leaders, sometimes large landowners in the district, played a much more important role, and very frequently it was they who also collected the taxes. Like the British and the Israelis after them, the Ottomans usually conducted what business they had with the villagers through *mukhtars*, who were government-appointed agents in the villages. One or several were chosen according to the size of the village and the number of *hamulas* or clans it had. Their job was essentially to represent the government's interests in the village, keep a record of births, deaths and migration and generally act as a kind of intermediary between villagers and the authorities.

Their effectiveness in fulfilling this role has always varied considerably. The British in the 1930s tried to strengthen their role, especially to include greater responsibilities for collection of taxes and fines. However, their efforts to make *mukhtars* more effective agents were foiled during the rebellions of 1936-9 when, particularly in areas where the government virtually lost control (for instance in the villages around Jenin, in Galilee, and the hills around Jerusalem), *mukhtars* were not in a comfortable position – under pressure to inform on villagers involved in 'subversion' but also under threat of losing their lives if they did

Otherwise the Mandate authorities' contact with villages was through district commissioners and their assistants, health, agriculture and education officers, and the police. As the situation in the countryside grew increasingly tense from the mid-1930s onwards, so British officialdom tended to retreat to the comparative safety of the cities.

Landowners

Another reason villages could never be seen as completely self-contained or autonomous was the subordination of their inhabitants, not just to the government of the day, but also to landowners, creditors and merchants. These are power relationships which one would be hard put to guess at from photographic evidence, except where violent physical clashes occurred. The exercise of direct physical violence, something it is possible to record on film, was not the norm, although tax and debt collectors during the Ottoman period did sometimes appear with armed men to add conviction to their demands. Palestine was never a land of vast agricultural estates but there were an increasing number of landowners who held substantial areas of land, though these were frequently scattered in fairly small parcels. By the end of the Ottoman period Turkish estimates of land in the hands of the largest landowners showed that average holdings for about 120 of these were about 9,000 dunums while the average peasant holding was in the region of 50-60 dunums.

2

*Kadourie Agricultural School, Tulkarm, established in 1931.
Technical and agricultural education received comparatively
scant attention. The Tulkarm school was established with a
bequest from Sir Elias Kadourie, who wanted a single school
to be set up for Jews and Arabs. Jewish insistence that all
Jewish education should be conducted in Hebrew, however, led
to the founding of two separate schools, this one being for Arab
students only.*

3

*As the note shows, these photographs were taken by Afif
Tannus, who was attached to the Kadourie school, but doing
work funded by the American Near East Foundation which
funded a scheme to give agricultural education to practicing
teachers in rural areas. Some of the photographs are shown
with their original captions – intended as part of a propaganda
film on their work. Tannus seems to have imbibed many of the
paternalist ideas common among the British (and Americans)
in a colonial setting. An air of tokenism is also evident. The
emphasis on 'self-help' can be less charitably interpreted as a
need to produce results on the cheap since funds available for
social services to the villages were very limited. He admits that
educational facilities were insufficient, but in the cleanliness
and health campaigns omits to mention the difficulties of
maintaining these newly prescribed standards in villages
without proper water supplies or sewage. It is also worth
noting that at the time the photos were taken, 1931-2,
peasants all over the country were being severely hit by a fall
in agricultural prices (a spin-off of the world trade recession)
and a series of bad harvests.*

The Pictures contained in this album have
been taken during our visits to the different
village schools where members of last year's
Teachers Class have been stationed.

The first few pages represent this year's
Teachers' Class at the Agricultural School of
Tulkarm.

It is hoped that with these pictures we
will begin the development of our local lantern
slides, to be shown to the Fellahin on our trips
to the villages. The appeal that the projection
of his life conditions on the screen will make
to the Fellah cannot be overestimated.

Of course, for this purpose the slides will
be so arranged and grouped as to best illustrate
an objective lesson we wish to drive home to the
Fellah.

Tulkarm,
July 1st, 1932

Afif I. Tannus

4
Suhmata (Acre subdistrict):
'The Effendis lead the way
on a road-building campaign.
The crowd enthusiastically
follows.' (see also p. 97).

5
Suhmata: 'The mountainside
conquered – and the way is
safe for themselves and their
animals coming loaded from
the fields!'

6
'The demand for education is
great in the Arab villages.
There is no place for these
[children] at the government
school and they seek the old
shaikh with his primitive
kuttub '

7
'Jura village: the schoolboys
and their teacher [at a
government school]. Note the
modern school building.'

8

'Jenin: the schoolboys on their cleanliness campaign in one of the neighbouring villages.'

9

'Sarafand [on the coast 20 miles south of Haifa]: the medical officer showing the women how to keep their homes and children clean.'

10

'Samakh [near Sarafand]: a modified form of [school] inspection. The Inspector of Education moulding the character of youngsters.'

Landowners' relationships with their tenants and sharecroppers varied a great deal. Sometimes ties were quite strong if the landowning family lived in the village or in a nearby small town. In the nineteenth century some major families could actually raise peasant militias from the villages they controlled. By the end of the century, though, the Ottoman authorities had managed to contain most of this faction fighting, and struggles for power between rival families took less violent forms. Among some of these families, even when many of their members went to live in the bigger towns, close ties with the villages remained. These ties represented a political power base and of course a major source of revenue, whether from rent (in kind or, by the 1930s, sometimes in money) or from the sale of the produce of the land.

Other landowners had no base in the rural areas, being merchants, money lenders or bankers who had acquired land as an investment or when a peasant had to give up land because of indebtedness. A vivid phrase was used of this – to become a 'partner of the wind' *(sharik al-huwa)*. *Sharik* was the word used for the contract relationship between tenant and landowner.

If changes in landholding patterns began in Ottoman times they accelerated rapidly during the Mandate. Few peasants sold their land to Jewish organisations or individuals directly in the 1920s. The high prices which did tempt some large landowners to part with some, if not all, of their land did not seem so attractive to smallholders for whom land was not simply a commodity or one among a number of forms of capital, but the only tangible asset they had. As such, few would risk parting company with their land unless indebtedness left them with no alternative or some attractive alternative source of livelihood presented itself. In the 1930s, more peasants sold out, both to Jewish and Arab buyers, impoverished by a series of bad seasons and the collapse in agricultural prices in the wake of the worldwide depression.

However, even in the 1920s some tenants and bedouin lost access to land they had tilled or used as pasturage when it changed hands. For sharecroppers or tenant farmers this did not always make much difference if the buyer was another Palestinian landowner, unless he wished to turn land over from small scale cultivation of field crops to plantation citriculture and employ wage labour instead of tenants or sharecroppers. If the buyer was Jewish, however, it almost always meant moving on, with or without compensation. Sometimes alternative land was offered, though not always in the same district. Peasants usually did not take kindly to being moved far away from their home district often to different sorts of land and cultivation. Land sold to the major Zionist land-buying institution during the Mandate – the Jewish National Fund – automatically became the 'inalienable property of the Jewish people', so no repurchase by Arabs or anyone else was possible.

The Citrus Business

The rapid development of citrus plantations exporting their produce to Europe was another factor which, beginning in the late nineteenth century, moved away from the village-based character of all other agricultural production. What eventually became standardised as the 'Jaffa orange' had already overtaken wheat, sesame and olives as Palestine's most important agricultural export before World War I. It was big business for both growers and exporters which continued to expand in area until the late 1930s.

At this time Jews and Arabs held fairly comparable shares of land under citrus (in 1934, 44% was Arab owned and 56% Jewish; in 1937-8, annual production from Jewish groves was 6,868,000 cases, from Arab groves 4,244,000 cases). However, Jewish marketing and packing was more centralised and better organised through a co-operative movement whereas most Arab owners still sold individually through about 270 different export agents. Furthermore, the more favourable long-term capital backing available to Jewish growers through Keren Hayesod, the financial arm of the Jewish National Fund, encouraged investment in more sophisticated equipment and irrigation systems.

Arab groves relied more heavily for their profit margins on the use of cheap labour. They were not alone in this, however. One of the conflicts which arose between Jewish grove owners and the Histadrut (Jewish trade union organisation) in the mid-1930s and even earlier was the latter's determination to enforce the use of Jewish labour only in the orange groves against the owners' desire to use (much cheaper) Arab labour in order to cut costs.

11

Orange grove at Bir Salem in Ramle subdistrict. In 1944, this village had 742 dunums of citrus (irrigated), 510 dunums of other irrigated crops and 1,468 dunums of field crops. In some villages on the coast the proportions were reversed, with more land under irrigation than under non-irrigated field crops. The young man in the tarbush is probably the owner of the grove, or a member of the owner's family.

12

12 13
Grading and wrapping
oranges. Much of the labour
force for this kind of work
was seasonal, employed from
about November to March.

13

Villagers Migrate

One solution to the problems of a peasant or a bedouin who had no land, or not enough to live on, who was chronically in debt or whose family could not afford to support him, was to leave the village or tent in search of a job elsewhere.

I say 'he' deliberately since few women left the village to work at this time. The only exception was the employment of village girls or women as servants or occasionally as wet nurses in more well-to-do families, and short spells of harvest work. Because most villagers at this time were illiterate or had limited education, the only kind of work they could take was manual and unskilled. Until the late 1920s, however, there were not all that many opportunities available. Before World War I there were very few, except at harvest time when it was possible for men and women to find daily paid work in the neighbourhood picking olives or fruit, or reaping. In the hills, people seeking such work would often go down to the plains where the crops ripened earlier, so that they could then return home in time to harvest their own crops.

Another way of fitting wage work into the seasonal pattern of agricultural life was to go and work in the citrus groves during the picking season, which ran from November to March and so did not interfere too much with the busy period in other types of agriculture which fell roughly between March to September. By the late 1920s large construction projects like Haifa harbour and road-building called for a lot of unskilled labour which attracted people from the villages even though the wages were very low. Since most villagers did not want entirely to give up their connection with their village and land (if they had any), the attraction was again that most of the work was on a short-term basis.

A small number of people found more regular work in factories or on the railways and some of these settled in town permanently or went home at intervals if they did not live too far away. Distance from the main towns and from centres of economic activity on the coast was clearly a major factor in determining whether or not people went away to work, but after 1930 there was a perceptible growth in the numbers of the more adventurous – or desperate – who came to the coast from places distant by Palestinian standards. A few villages had work conveniently on their doorstep in the shape of army camps or roads being built close by, for which contractors would usually try to hire labour from nearby villages through the agency of *mukhtar*s or other village notables.

What precise social or political impact this growth in migrant labour had on villages is hard to judge. Most migrants remained in close touch with their villages and many, working in citrus groves or on the roads, would not have been much in contact with town life. For those who actually did spend time in cities like Jaffa or Haifa the political and social impact would probably have been greater.

It may be that the political atmosphere in the cities influenced at least some of these migrants to question, more than most villagers were accustomed to do, the social and economic structures which prevailed in the countryside. The threat posed by Zionism and British support for it may also have appeared more vivid when the growth of Jewish settlement in cities and countryside on the coast was seen at close quarters.

Palestine wage levels 1928

Unskilled labour:

Jewish unionised	250–300 mils per day
Jewish nonunionised	150–300 mils per day
Arab urban	140–170 mils per day
Arab rural	120–150 mils per day

Report of the Palestine Government Wages Commission, 1928

'I remained in the village [his own village] for about 15 days when a person from Kalkilia, Husein Abu Aba, a contractor, came and engaged 20 persons and me among them, to work in stone cutting near Kalkilia. I worked there for 20 days. On finishing the work I returned to Silet el Dahr. I stayed three days in the village when Amin Umrad of my family received a letter from Dib el Kaled of Tyre, a contractor, living in Haifa, asking him to come with 2 workmen to work in Haifa. I proceeded to Haifa where I worked for the said contractor in the drainage [sic] for about a month. I left then in order to return to my village and buy corn for the family.'
(Statement of evidence when questioned by police about involvement in guerrilla activities by Abdul Rahim Abdul Karim abu Diyyak, 2 May 1938. From a document on the Tegart papers, Middle East Centre, Oxford.)

Proceedings of a Congress of Arab Villagers

On November 5 and 6, 1929, an assembly of over 300 Arab peasants met in Jaffa to discuss conditions affecting the Palestine farmers. This was the first meeting of its kind ever held in Palestine.

Among those representatives present were the following Effendis, who are all of peasant origin, born in villages, but who acquired some education and have adopted the European mode of dress.

1. Abdel Kader Effendi el-Shible, an advocate of Acre, who acted as chairman of the Congress. He was born at El Makre village, near Acre, and is a landowner. He is married to a village woman. He is the official representative of the Acre Village Union, which includes 45 villages.

2. Abdel Muti el-Barghouthi, representative of Deir Ghasaneh village and a landowner.

3. Tewfik Effendi Naser, representing villages around Jaffa.

4. Kamel al-Kadi, representing Tarshiba village, and who is an important tobacco grower.

5. Hafez Abu Bakir, representative of Baka el-Gharbieh (village) in the Nablus district.

The following named representatives are purely peasants but are notables in their villages:

1. Muhammad Effendi Hamadeh, representing Shafa Amr district which includes 10 villages.

2. Selem el-Tiby, representative of the Villages Union Association of Jaffa district

3. El-Sheikh Hussain Hassouneh, representing the Young Men's Village Association at Ludd (Lydda).

4. El-Sheikh Suleiman, representing Fajeh and Kufr Am in Ramle district.

According to the Arab press the following conclusions were reached by the Congress:

1. That the economic condition of the arab farmer is very poor; the gross annual income per family not exceeding LP 25.000 ($ 125); of this amount more than 12 % is paid out in taxes and as the remainder is insufficient for the support of the family and to cover operating expenses, it becomes necessary to borrow at high rates of interest. Unemployment in the villages is steadily increasing partly due to preferential treatment of Jewish labor by the Government. In view of these conditions, the Congress proposes:

(a) That the minimum gross income of the farmer should be LP 60.000 per year including operating expenses, and that this minimum income should be exempt from taxation.

(b) That the Government should liquidate the debts of the farmers and establish an agricultural bank without delay.

---

arab villagers 2

(c) That the farmer should be protected by proper legislation from selling the land which is essential to his living.

(d) That more peasants should be employed by the Government in public works.

(e) That the budget of the Department of Agriculture should be increased in order to permit an increase in the number of experimental farms and to assist the farmers in tree planting.

(f) That the Government should effectively prohibit exorbitant rates of interest.

2. That the country cannot stand any further taxation; at the same time the heavy expenditures of the Government can be greatly reduced if the policy based on the Balfour Declaration is given up. Finding that the greater part of the present unsatisfactory economic conditions in Palestine are (sic) due to the policy maintained as a result of the Balfour Declaration, the Congress voted to request the abrogation of that Declaration and a change in policy.

3. That the sanitary conditions of Arab villages, especially as regards their water supply, is deplorable and that the Government has thus far done very little to ameliorate these conditions, although it has recently cancelled a debt of the Municipality of Tel Aviv (Jewish) of LP 75.000.
The Congress therefore voted to request the appropriation of Government funds for the improvement of every Arab village and the establishment of additional medical stations in each subdistrict.

4. That although Arab villages are ready and willing to assist in the construction of village roads, the Government fails to render them proper assistance while it treats the Jewish colonies in a preferential manner in this respect and does not employ them without pay as it does in the case of the Arabs.
The Congress therefore voted to request that the Government participate in the construction of village roads in Arab villages.

5. To request that village schools be greatly increased and that training in the schools be based on agriculture.

A report by the United States Consul in Jerusalem, Harry Troutman, to the State Department. The 'villagers' represented here seem mostly to be either landowners with strong village connections or richer peasants. However, the criticisms voiced here were undoubtedly among the major preoccupations of many people in the rural areas at this time.

1

Bedouin woman and child outside their tent. The heavy woven material suspended from the tent roof was probably made by the bedouin themselves. The women wove heavy fabrics from wool and goats' hair for hangings, rugs, bags and camel saddles on large horizontal ground looms.

2

Bedouin shaikhs in Jerusalem. Bedouin came into the cities periodically either to negotiate with or petition the government of the day or to trade.

3 THE BEDOUIN

Bedouin life probably underwent more fundamental changes during the period following World War I than did that of any other section of the population. National boundaries, strengthened central government control, and the constant shrinking of the amount of land available as pasturage all affected the bedouin's ability to survive economically in the ways to which they had been accustomed in Turkish times.

The particular attention which some European writers and photographers paid to bedouin in preference to peasants or townspeople tends to leave an impression that they formed a larger part of the population than they actually did. The 1931 census, probably the most accurate count made, gave the number of bedouin as 66,553 – 6.4% of the total population and 8% of the Muslim population. Of these 70% lived in the south, in the Beersheba region, and 10% lived in the Dead Sea area. The rest were dispersed through the north – in Beisan, Galilee, the plain of Esdraelon and the coastal plain.

By the onset of the twentieth century very few of these bedouin, who usually lived in fairly small clan or family groups (although a few clans were up to 1,000 strong), were 'pure' nomads. In other words, although they lived in tents and raised animals, they usually also cultivated some crops, though this might be sporadic. They seldom migrated far from their base area, in contrast to some of the bedouin tribes of the Syrian desert and of Arabia. In the north, the tendency to stay in one place was still more marked and many of the small tribes or clans living in Galilee or in the plains became very little different in their economic lifestyle from their peasant neighbours. Most bedouin still lived in tents, though in some places the black goats' hair of which they were traditionally made was giving way to sacking and other materials. Their social customs still differed in some respects from those of the village but even here the gap narrowed.

Social contact with villagers probably increased as bedouin power declined and raids on villages became less common. Some semi-settled groups intermarried with villagers. In late Ottoman times, among villagers in the Bethlehem area, men of the semi-settled Ta'amri tribe were considered good 'catches' as husbands since like all bedouin they were not obliged to do military service. They were therefore not liable to be spirited away from the village for unpredictable periods.

3
Bedouin of southern Palestine who lived in the area from Beersheba down to the Gulf of Aqaba, in which there was little other settlement.

4

Originally entitled 'Dipping hands in the dish', this photograph shows bedouin men and children sitting around a pottery dish which looks empty. They are probably simply posed by the photographer and not actually eating. In the long tent, only part of which is visible, the women's section was divided from the men's. The latter was where guests were received.

5

Bedouin children from the north, near Lake Tiberias. The younger child is wearing a tiny blue bead (which looks like a small white dot under the headcloth) for protection against the 'evil eye'. The wearing of blue beads for this reason was common among both bedouin and peasants. The 'eye' was the representation of the ill-will or jealousy of others which, it was considered, could blight a person's life and was much feared.

84

6

Bedouin buying grain from a peasant.

The imposition of relatively strong centralised rule deprived the bedouin of political power, which under the Turks had been exercised through tribal chiefs *(shaikhs)* who, if they led a large and powerful tribe, often held considerable sway locally – sometimes more than the Turkish authorities. In the long run, the authority of the *shaikhs* with their own people also diminished, since it was no longer in their power to defend the tribe and make it prosper.

Certain activities which had contributed to the bedouin economy in earlier days were gradually halted. One was the growing and sale of tobacco. This was stopped before the British came with the imposition of the 'Régie de Tabac' (Tobacco Monopoly) in 1883. During the Mandate bedouin were also barred from selling salt which they used to collect from the salt pans around the Dead Sea and in the Sinai peninsular and sell in the markets of Gaza, Ramle, Nablus and other towns. They had often bartered salt for wheat, barley and other necessities. In Ottoman times most bedouin were armed and the arms trade was another part of their livelihood. Although the British clamped down on the trade, there can be little doubt that this and other kinds of smuggling did continue.

For those who lived in the northern half of the country new problems arose. Particularly in the plains where the demand for land for Jewish settlement was greatest, the bedouin, who seldom had any kind of formal rights to the land they used for grazing or for cultivation, tended to be pushed from one place to another as land was transferred to Jewish colonies – either through concessions granted on State lands (i.e. land not registered as being under regular cultivation or specifically registered as the property of the State) or by the sale of private lands on which bedouin had previously been allowed to graze their flocks or cultivate crops. Like landless peasants, numbers of bedouin became wage labourers. Under these sorts of pressure the close knit clan units began to break up economically and then socially.

The British did not have a policy of systematically breaking up bedouin society or forcing settlement as did the French in Syria, but the changing economic structure in Palestine over which they presided did not leave space or freedom for nomadic society to maintain the strength or autonomy it had enjoyed under the Ottomans.

7
Washing camels on the Palestine coast. Although some bedouin turned to agriculture and wage labour, herds of camels were still considered an important form of wealth.

8

A bedouin (with rifle slung over his shoulder) smoking a clay pipe with a long wooden stem while the man on the left plays a rababeh – a kind of one-stringed lute. One pre-World War I European observer records that these pipes (ralyoun) were by then only smoked by bedouin and a few older peasants. They had been more common before the imposition of the tobacco *'régie' in 1883. Commercially manufactured cigarettes became more popular during the Mandate when a number of cigarette factories were established. The location is on the road from Jerusalem to Jericho at the so-called Good Samaritan Inn. The people in the foreground may have been posed there to add interest to the photograph.*

1

The arrival in Jaffa of the
first British High
Commissioner, Sir Herbert
Samuel, in 1920. Ships
could not anchor close inshore
and all passengers and goods
had to be ferried by boat from
beyond the line of rocks seen
here to the shore. In bad
weather this could be
dangerous (see p. 105). All
the boatmen here are wearing
shirts emblazoned with the
intitials OETA (Occupied
Enemy Territory
Administration), the British
military administration in
Palestine from 1917, from
which Samuel took over.

2

Camel pulling a baggage
wagon at Lydda airport
(1937), the kind of scene
much beloved of
photographers of the Third
World to this day – the
bizarre, and to western eyes
improbable, juxtaposition of
'traditional' and 'modern'.
Whether, in fact, the use of
camels was normal practice at
that time, or whether there
was some passing shortage of
other baggage pullers, is not
known.

4   MOVING AROUND

The tightening of bonds between city and village and between Palestine and the rest of the world was in part the result of improved communications. In 1880 tourists travelled around the country at the staid pace of a horse. In 1938 D. G. Salameh, Thomas Cook's chief agent in Jerusalem, commented in disapproving terms:

> With the introduction of the motor car, the old aspect of visiting the Holy Land has changed. Instead of a leisurely visit of practically all places of interest in Jerusalem and the surrounding country the average visitor nowadays is content to rush through the country at the rate of 40 miles an hour spending perhaps 3 or 4 days for the whole of Palestine. The advantages of quick transition from point to point seem to have outweighed in the majority of cases, the other advantages of really learning something of the country, the inhabitants, and their mode of life. I regard it as most unfortunate that the average traveller these days seems to be willing to take a glance at Palestine, in passing as it were, and without any intelligent appreciation of the manifold subtleties of life here and the fact that Palestine is a mirror of civilization dating back thousands of years.

(Arab Chambers of Commerce, *Directory of Arab Trade, Industry, Crafts and Professions*, Jerusalem, 1938, p. 40–41).

Whether or not the slowness of nineteenth century journeys actually had much influence in heightening the visitor's social awareness of Palestinian life is, however, a moot point.

3

A postcard produced in Jerusalem commemorating the first Turkish airman to fly into Palestine and over Jerusalem during World War I – Fathi Bey. The card is in Ottoman Turkish, except for the little heading added over the top of the photographs which says 'martyrs of the nation' in Arabic.

4

*Imperial Airways flight at
Lydda airport. The
ambulance in the foreground
belongs to the Jewish, not
government, health services.*

5

*Jerusalem railway station,
with its sign in English,
Arabic and Hebrew.*

6
Village women returning home from market in Jerusalem.

7
The National Bus Company running a service from Tel Aviv via Jerusalem to Beirut (1934). It also ran regular services from Jaffa to Jerusalem and Jerusalem to Haifa. A few taxi services also operated on a long-distance basis.

8
A dramatic night shot by Matson. Villagers in al-Khadr (Jerusalem subdistrict) listening to the radio of a passing car. At that time (October 1937) the rebellion was beginning to take hold in the rural areas and the British placed restrictions on movement. Radios were therefore an increasingly important source of news as well as entertainment.

9
A film show in Halhul, near Hebron in July 1940. The 'screen' was the wall of the mosque. Most of the films would have been from Britain or from Hollywood. One of Matson's night photographs.

Cartoon translated from the Arabic Jaffa newspaper Filastin in 1936 portraying the effect on Jews (mice in hats) and Arabs (cats in kuffirs) of a speech by the British Colonial Secretary broadcast on the radio.
Below:
programmes from the Palestine Broadcasting Service for 1 May 1936. The programmes aimed at Arabic-speaking listeners are underscored. The principal broadcasting station was in Ramalla, north of Jerusalem.

The Whole Object !!!

« The whole object of His Britannic Majesty's Government is that both Arabs and Jews should be able to live together in peace and amity.....»

« From Colonial Secretary's speech » broadcasted

Wireless Programmes
Today and Tomorrow
PALESTINE TIME

FRIDAY
PALESTINE BROADCASTING SERVICE

5.30 p.m. Announcements, 5.35 p.m. Arabic Children's Corner.

6.00 p.m. Stories to Village Listeners (A); 6.15 p.m. Haj Rizq al Yafawi and the Studio Group (Leader: Jamil 'Uweis); 6.30 p.m. News in Arabic; 6.35 p.m. Concert of Symphonic Music (∅).

7.05 p.m. Humorous Monologues by Rifqi and 'Abdallah with the Studio Group; 7.40 p.m. "Qeis and Yaman" by 'Omar Saleh el Barghuthi (A);

7.55 p.m. News in English, Arabic and Hebrew.

8.10 p.m. Hebrew Reading; 8.15 p.m. Hebrew Calendar; 8.20 p.m. "Jews in Russia" by Dan Pines (H); 8.30 p.m. Reading by S. Kutal (H); 8.40 p.m. English Keyboard Music from Byrd to Bax (The Third of a Series of Recitals by Sydney Seal (Pianoforte).

9.00 p.m. Old English Songs by Rachel Maud Chinn At the Piano: Sydney Seal; 9.20 p.m. Yahya es Sg'udi and the Studio Group (Leader: Jamil 'Uweis). 9.50 p.m. Concert of Chamber Music (∅).

10.30 p.m. Close Down.

93

For Palestinians, journeys were often undertaken on foot, otherwise on horse or donkey-back, according to the status of the person concerned. By the middle of the Mandate period, however, bus or even car travel had become an option. Private cars were still comparatively rare but a number of taxi and car hire firms were in business.

These changes encouraged mobility, whether for work or social visits, and combined with the fairly widespread introduction of telephones in business premises and wealthy homes, they also contributed to the quickening pace of political life.

Co-ordination of political activity on a national level was made easier and news of incidents in one part of the country quickly reached others. Broadcasting and more widespread distribution of newspapers were also contributing factors.

The Turks had gradually improved the communications network in the years before World War I. The railway from Jaffa to Jerusalem, after some hitches, was built by a French company and opened in 1892. This both increased the pilgrim and tourist traffic to Jerusalem and contributed to the expansion and prosperity of small

10
Jewish workers building a road from Netanya to Tulkarm (1935). At an earlier period, during the 1927-9 recession in the Jewish economy, there was widespread Jewish unemployment and the British administration came under heavy pressure from the Jewish Agency to support road-building programmes around Jewish colonies, not just for strategic reasons, but as a way of providing employment for new immigrants and existing Jewish unemployed.

11
Bonfils photograph of Druze children in Ottoman times carrying stones for a road on Mount Carmel. Roadmaking was then a form of compulsory labour. The British introduced a law in 1927 which, though not abolishing the labour requirement, stipulated that a rate or tax could be paid in lieu.

12

Camel caravan on the Jaffa-Jerusalem road. In Ottoman times wheeled transport was not very common and was also expensive. On this road, the tolls levied were reported by British consular sources in the 1880s to be as follows: the equivalent of 2/8d for a carriage or cart; 3½d for a camel; 2½d for a pack horse or mule; 1½d for a donkey.

towns en route – particularly Lydda and Ramle. More roads were built in the late nineteenth century but most were poorly maintained and this discouraged wheeled transport. During the war the Turks were spurred to further railway-building efforts by the need to transport their troops. The British during the Mandate showed on the whole more interest in roads than in railways though they retained most of the railway system the Ottomans had created. Road building concentrated in the main on major arterial roads and smaller roads linking Jewish colonies on the coastal plain to major highways. The Zionist Organisation provided up to three-quarters of the finance for the colony roads and the Administration provided the remainder.

13
Camel carrying stone blocks for building in Jerusalem.

14
Although the bulk of citrus was packed in crates and shipped to Europe in large steamers, the coastal trade in oranges and other goods continued in these small sailing boats, though their share of total trade dwindled drastically afer World War I.

15
Citrus for export to Europe. Total exports from Jewish and Arab groves reached 15.3 million cases in 1938-9. Citrus had first become an important export in the 1880s and by 1904 467,000 cases were exported.

*Haifa harbour,
Britain's largest public works
venture during the Mandate,
was built by the government
Public Works Department
and completed in October
1933.*

Elsewhere village roads were supposed to be built by local people using their own labour. This rule was only broken during the rebellion period from 1936 to 1939 when the British built some roads in the hill districts, not for the improvement of the area, but to improve access for the military who were attempting to quell the rebellion.

The rapid growth of both imports and exports before World War I centred not on the old camel caravan trade routes to Syria, Iraq and the Hijaz but on seaborne trade with Europe. Oranges, sesame and olive oil went by steamship to Liverpool, Marseilles and other European ports while manufactured goods, especially Manchester cottons, woollen and silk goods, hardware and glassware, were offloaded at Jaffa. Trade in this direction swelled still further after the war with imports far outpacing exports. The opening of Haifa harbour in 1933 furthered this growth in foreign trade and threatened to eclipse Jaffa as a port as the latter still only had very limited facilities.

Transport of goods inside the country became slowly and patchily motorised. Until the 1940s lorries were far more common in the Jewish sector, their expense being beyond the means of most smaller Palestinian farmers and businessmen. Camels remained an important part of the landscape – not, as now, posing for tourists – but as a relatively cheap means of bulk transport. In fact an increase in the import of camels (bred mostly by the bedouin of Transjordan and Syria) for use in the building trade – transporting stone, sand and other materials – was reported even in the 1920s. Camels also continued to be used for carrying bulk agricultural goods. Merchants would sometimes keep strings of camels for their own use and to hire out. Sometimes they would employ a professional camel driver who would be encouraged to work well and stay in the job by being given a share in the capital invested in the camels. Later on, when lorries began to replace the camels, similar sorts of arrangements were made.

Communications also had an important bearing on the reasons for Britain's interest in holding onto Palestine, unrewarding as it sometimes appeared in other respects. Haifa harbour and Lydda airport were both important for military purposes – the first because it was the only deep water port under British control on the eastern Mediterranean coast. Haifa was also the terminal of the vital pipeline from the Iraqi oilfields. Lydda was a useful staging post for military as well as civil aircraft on the route to Iraq and thence to India. Britain also controlled land routes from Palestine on the Mediterranean, through Transjordan to Iraq and the Arabian/Persian Gulf. All these factors were to pay considerable strategic and military dividends during World War II.

5   THE ECONOMY
OF CITIES AND TOWNS

Photographers' Views of Towns

For photographers the visual attractions of town life in Palestine were of a different order from those of the countryside. The interest of visiting photographers centred on Jerusalem, for its historical and biblical associations and, for some, though not all, for what they saw as its beauty. Other smaller towns like Nazareth and Bethlehem came in for a good deal of attention because of their Christian religious associations but the Muslim towns of the interior – notably Nablus and Hebron – were rarely visited or photographed. Nablus was usually only on the itinerary to be passed en route to the Samaritan holy places nearby. The old port town of Jaffa was usually a stopover place for seaborne visitors before setting off for Jerusalem and received fairly cursory photographic treatment.

Even a professional photographer like Eric Matson, who lived in Palestine for many years and whose pictures cover an unusually wide range of places and activities, placed the greatest stress on Jerusalem. In the old city, the bustling life in the streets, the mix of people (or 'types' as they were often called) and the glimpses of private life in almost concealed houses and courtyards were sources of fascination. For those with any pretensions to photographic skill, the play of light and shadow, the faces, the shapes in the narrow streets and arched *suq*s (markets) were a technical challenge not to be missed.

A sense of strangeness, a choosing of what seemed odd and different, was very much in evidence. Even scenes or events which would seem quite unremarkable to a local inhabitant would appear different and exotic. There is no shortage, for instance, of views of shops and workshops, open to the street and functioning in ways unfamiliar to Europeans. Hence photographers recorded numerous beaming shopkeepers and merchants, posed before their 'exotic' wares. Small craftsmen were similarly recorded. While they did not usually carry the baggage of biblical associations which attached to ploughmen, shepherds and fishermen, these photographs create the same sense of singularity and isolation which make it hard to picture the social and economic context in which the merchant, craftsmen, porter or water seller lived.

1 2

Street scenes, in Jerusalem. On the right, George Adam Smith, author of several books on Palestine, *experiments with an early wide-angle lens in one of a whole series of panoramas of Jerusalem.*

3

4

3
Jerusalem under snow in 1920. Winter in the hills did not always bring snow, but cold winds and rain were common from November to March. In photographs from Jerusalem and the other hill towns it is often possible to tell the time of year from people's clothing. On the coast this does not apply, since it seldom got very cold.

4
A Palestinian peasant woman and her baby in Nahalat Binyamin Street, Tel Aviv (1935). Tel Aviv lay adjacent to Jaffa but only a handful of Arabs lived there (see table). Note that the woman is wearing a European-style checked cotton dress under her embroidered over-dress.

Both this attitude and the interest in technically beautiful pictures meant that urban poverty was, if not romanticised, at least smoothed into picturesqueness. There is little of the fascination with poverty 'as a way of life' which is to be found in the photographic studies of slums and shanty towns in Europe and the USA from the early twentieth century. The shanty towns of Haifa and Jaffa in the 1930s did not attract such concern, but, since 1948, refugee camps have come nearest to attracting this kind of attention.

On the whole, photographs of newer towns like Haifa or Tel Aviv tended to show less fascination with the 'quaint' ways of their people and more interest in their expansion and 'progress'.

4

The Growth of Towns

If it is sometimes difficult to make generalisations about rural life, this is even more of a problem when looking at towns, each of which had its own specific identity, historical pattern of growth and economic importance. One thing is clear, however, and is interestingly expressed in the table, that even in the first ten years of the Mandate, the shift in the balance of population between urban centres – both large and small – was quite striking.

The most obvious fact is the rapid increase in the populations of the four largest towns – Jerusalem, Haifa, Jaffa and Tel Aviv. Of course, in talking about the Palestinian population alone, these figures are distorting because quite a large proportion of the overall increase is the result of Jewish immigration. Tel Aviv was an almost exclusively Jewish town and just one third of the population of Haifa in 1931 was Jewish. Jerusalem had a long established Jewish community and this was added to by post-World War I immigration. Jaffa, however, was a mainly Arab town throughout the period.

Comparable growth rates in the smaller towns in the first ten years of the Mandate (for instance over 35%) are only to be found in Tulkarm, Beisan, Lydda and Ramle (all of which had immigrant populations) and Ramalla, a prosperous Christian village which grew into a small town during the Mandate (not all of these towns are shown in the table). Other towns actually lost population or had minimal growth (Gaza, Nablus, Hebron, Safad, Bethlehem, Khan Yunis, Beit Jala and Jenin). In some, though not all of these, it is interesting to note that the growth rate for men is much lower than that for women, which might imply that men were leaving to seek work elsewhere. By the 1940s, the overall drift to the cities, immigration and a high birth rate had swelled all urban populations.

Emigration from Palestine by Palestinians was not all that common during the Mandate though it was more frequent in the last years of Turkish rule. Substantially more Christians emigrated than Muslims, very often going to the USA, like their co-religionists from Lebanon, who were emigrating to the USA, South America and West Africa in large numbers at the beginning of the century.

5

Nablus, never a magnet for tourists, was nevertheless an important provincial town in the nineteenth century and a centre of nationalist activity during the Mandate, though its economic position declined relative to that of the coastal towns.

Jaffa, landing place
Jaffa, Landungsplatz
Jaffa, la rade

6 *A souvenir postcard view of the landing place at Jaffa. The town was largely rebuilt at the beginning of the nineteenth century after Napoleon's occupation of 1799 had reduced much of it to ruins.*

Population of major towns, 1922, 1931 (census counts) and 1944 (estimate)

Town	*1922* *total population* of which:*	*Jews* *Muslims* *Christians*	*1931* *total population* of which:*	*Jews* *Muslims* *Christians*	*% change 1922/31*	*1944* *total population* of which:*	*Jews* *Muslims* *Christians*	*% change 1931/44*
Jerusalem	62,578	33,971 13,413 14,699	90,503	51,222 19,894 19,335	+44.6	157,080	97,000 30,630 29,350	+73.6
Haifa	24,634	6,230 9,377 8,863	50,403	15,923 20,401 13,827	+104.6	128,800	66,000 35,940 26,570	+155.5
Jaffa	32,524	5,087 20,621 6,808	51,866	7,209 35,506 9,132	+59.5	94,310	28,000 50,880 15,400	+81.8
Tel Aviv	15,185	15,065 78 42	46,101	45,564 106 143	+203.6	166,660	166,000 130 230	+261.5
Gaza	17,480	54 16,722 701	17,046	1 16,356 689	−2.5	34,170	0 33,160 1,010	+100.5
Nablus	15,947	16 15,238 544	17,189	6 16,483 533	+7.8	23,250	0 22,360 680	+35.3
Hebron	16,577	430 16,074 73	17,531	135 17,276 112	+5.8	24,560	0 24,400 150	+40.1
Lydda	8,103	11 7,166 926	11,250	28 10,002 1,210	+38.8	16,780	20 14,910 1,840	+49.2
Ramle	7,312	35 5,837 1,440	10,421	8 8,211 2,200	+42.5	15,160	0 11,900 3,260	+45.6

*where a discrepancy exists between total population and the break down into Jews, Muslims and Christians totalled this is described in the figures as 'others' and refers primarily to Palestine's Druze community.

(*Census of Palestine 1922*; *Census of Palestine 1931*; 1944 population estimate in *Survey of Palestine* 1946).

Most of those who left their home towns would have been more likely to go to one of the large towns to look for work. This signalled some change in the role of towns as centres for trade, mainly in agricultural products, of small scale crafts and in some cases, of administration. Trade and services began to take on a different complexion, larger scale industry developed and living styles changed.

A 'national'-scale market also developed as both locally made and imported manufactured goods were more widely distributed. Goods previously easily available only in the area where they were made could be had in most parts of the country, although individual towns still remained famous for particular products – Nablus and Jaffa for soap, Hebron for glass, Gaza for black pottery and rugs, Majdal for weaving, Bethlehem for mother-of-pearl work, and so on. Prices of goods, whether manufactured or agricultural, still varied early in the Mandate according to area and proximity to the source of supply. Thus, the *Commercial Bulletin* reported in 1923 that soap was cheapest in Nablus, olives in Nablus and Acre, charcoal in Jenin, wheat and bread in Gaza   elsewhere transport costs could increase the price several times over.

Currency also became standardised during the Mandate. Under the British, first the Egyptian pound and then the Palestinian pound became the legal tender. The value of both was linked to the pound sterling. This was a considerable change from the Ottoman period when a bewildering variety of coinage was considered legal tender. Baedeker's guide *Palestine et Syrie* in 1912 recorded that in Turkish currency there were three copper coins, five silver, one gold (the Turkish lira) and seven other metal *(metalik)* pieces in use in Palestine, each of which had a different value in Jerusalem and in Jaffa. In addition, French francs, English pounds, Russian roubles and Austrian schillings were also common currency. Paper money, first introduced during World War I, was profoundly distrusted and took some time to gain acceptance outside the main towns.

Jerusalem and the Pilgrim Trade

Jerusalem, though much changed in some respects after the Ottomans left, retained its main characteristics as a centre of administration, of religious affairs, of pilgrimage and of tourism. This character of a service city, rather than a centre of industry or trade, essentially remains to this day.

A certain number of people were employed in the Ottoman and then the British administration and another group by the plethora of religious organisations, Christian and Muslim, which were housed there. Greek Orthodox, Catholic, Protestant, Copt and Armenian – all had various kinds and sizes of churches, convents, charitable foundations and hospices. Most sects also had the care of holy places or corners of holy places. Muslim religious organisation was rather more coherent since Sunni Islam was the dominant persuasion of Muslim Palestinians and there was therefore no sectarian conflict over control of the Muslim holy places – most notably the Haram ash-Sharif. Where conflicts arose, both here and in the Mosque of Abraham in Hebron, they were mainly over competing claims to control over holy spots between Muslims and Jews. The Wailing Wall area, directly backing on to the Haram ash-Sharif, and the Mosque of Abraham were, of course, the scene of violent political/religious confrontations during the Mandate. Like Christian organisations, Muslim foundations also controlled charitable trusts, soup kitchens for the poor and various educational and health institutions. Most important was the administration of the Awqaf or religious endowments. They were controlled by a Ministry of Awqaf under the Ottomans and by the Supreme Muslim Council under the British and were of substantial economic worth, mainly in the form of property, urban and rural.

Pilgrimage and tourism, or rather the trade and services which they generated, were probably the largest source of income and employment. This was certainly the case before World War I when not only was there a growing number of more affluent tourists and/or pilgrims from Western Europe and the US, but the annual tide of Russian pilgrims was at its height. Unlike the former, the Russians were mostly poor peasants. Like many Muslim pilgrims to Mecca *(hajjis)* they would have saved up all their lives to make this journey. They came in large groups and stayed mostly in the hospices built by the Russian Orthodox Church. However, by the beginning of the 1900s the numbers were so great (reaching 10,000 annually in the years before 1914) that they could not all be accommodated there. They were often very badly swindled by the steamer companies which carried them, by local shopkeepers and by their own priests who also had an eye to the profits of the pilgrimage. Not that the pilgrims had much money, but their sheer numbers generated a need for services, foodstuffs and small souvenirs – icons, candles, little pious objects in olive wood and mother-of-pearl, and shrouds which they wore to be dipped in the Jordan River at Epiphany. The cutting off of the Russian traffic and indeed most other tourist traffic at the beginning of World War I was a considerable blow to numbers of Jerusalemites who had depended on this trade for their livelihoods. Other towns through which pilgrims usually passed – Jaffa, Lydda, Ramle, Bethlehem – were similarly affected.

The number of service activities generated by tourists, pilgrims and the general growth of trade before World War I was considerably influenced by the increasing importance of European consulates. In the first place these, like the religious establishments, required servants, cooks, messengers and guards. The spread of European influence had another significance. Immunities accorded under the Ottoman Capitulations were extended to local people who were working for or under the protection of a consul. These were usually Christians, who were more likely at that time to have contact with Europeans and to speak a European language. Thus in towns where Europeans had consular and business interests – mainly Jaffa, Haifa and Jerusalem – there developed a small class of mainly Christian businessmen and merchants whose role was to act as agents for and look after the interests of European commercial houses. Others worked directly for the consulates as interpreters or dragomen.

The growth of foreign trade boosted the prosperity of the ports along the coast, with the exception of Acre which lost its position to nearby Haifa which, scarcely more than a village in the late nineteenth century, became the most thriving commercial centre in Palestine by the 1930s. Acre had been a major outlet for grain from northern Palestine and from parts of Syria but its decline was ensured by the construction of a branch line off the Hijaz Railway from Damascus to Haifa which diverted the flow of grain and other exports.

8

'Sulaiman Girby – boatman of Jaffa', a photograph by D. Subrinji. Estelle Blyth, daughter of the Anglican Bishop Blyth of Jerusalem, appended the following story to this studio portrait: 'Girby was head boatman to Messrs Thomas Cook and Son. He was a magnificent oarsman, and saved many lives, landing in rough seas at Jaffa, where the reef of rocks made winter landings very dangerous. Amongst those whom he saved were Bishop Blyth and members of his family: and Sir George Newnes founder of [Newnes] Publishing Company and of the Strand Magazine. Sir George sent him from England a gold watch, inscribed. The then Turkish governor of Jaffa coveted the watch and asked Sulaiman for it several times: and as he refused to give it the Pasha sent him to prison on a trumped up charge. As Sulaiman still refused [sic], he was sent up to Jerusalem to prison, where he literally pined for the sea: he was allowed out on daily parole, and spent many of his days at the Bishop's house and he gave this photograph to Mrs Blyth. When the Pasha left Jaffa, Sulaiman was sent back to Jaffa at once. He, and his two brothers (only less good boatmen than he) died of cholera in the epidemic that swept Jaffa and Galilee (chiefly Caesarea and Tiberias) about 1905.'

9
Coppersmith at work.

Crafts

Craft industries were found in most Palestinian towns, large and small, but suffered from a similar process of erosion and change as has been experienced by small-scale hand manufacture in other colonial and semi-colonial countries. European machine-manufactured goods gradually poached away local markets and left the craftsmen to specialise or go out of business.

In a few cases in Palestine, local industries temporarily held their own by producing goods not usually made by European factories. The main surviving centre of weaving, Majdal, produced materials particularly suited to clothing worn by the peasantry – heavy wool fabric and indigo-dyed cotton for dresses, though mostly using imported yarn. To make these, the fabrics normally imported were not so suitable. However, photo-graphs show a gradual increase in the wearing of European-style shirts, trousers, jackets and other garments, whether ready-made or locally tailored from foreign fabrics. In the long run this trend undercut the local weaver.

Goods originally produced for use by the local population – pottery, rugs, dresses and glassware, for example – have been transformed into tourist souvenirs to the point where, today, many of these goods have no other markets at all. A few other trades, like mother-of-pearl work and olive and oak wood carving of religious mementos, were from the first directed at pilgrims and tourists. The growth in the overall size of the domestic market during the Mandate did little to help these industries as both Jewish immigrants and some wealthier urban Palestinians tended to favour European-style factory-produced goods.

10
Wheel-made, kiln-fired pottery, unlike the hand-built pots women made in the villages, was a commercial craft – and a male preserve. The range of pots, dishes and jars made was primarily for domestic use.

11
Jerusalem faience work; these painted and decorated wares are now produced mostly for tourists. Domestic pottery and copper vessels were gradually replaced by imported hardware, china and glassware.

12

12

Treadle looms in Majdal near Gaza. Though weaving continued on a small scale in other towns and villages, Majdal was the only remaining weaving centre of any importance in Palestine by the twentieth century. Even here the craft was declining: in 1909 there were an estimated 500 looms in the town, but by the 1930s this figure had declined to 200.

13 14

The weekly market at Majdal, selling local and imported materials, and an Armenian woman in Al Arish during World War I making clothes for refugees. Sewing machines were beginning to enter the market by this time, being used by tailors and dressmakers. Later, previously hand-sewn 'traditional' dresses began to be made up by machine.

13

14

15
Glass-making – the speciality of Hebron – was also overtaken by the competition of imported glassware, and the craftsmen turned instead to making vases, beads, bracelets, flower pots and cups for tourists. Before World War I, however, Hebron glass had been popular in the domestic market and was exported to Syria, Turkey, Egypt and even as far afield as

Rumania. There were said to have been seven factories (workshops of about the size seen here) but only one remained in 1938. Methods of production remained simple: the combination of local sand and an alkali. Hebron glass was also distinctively coloured, mostly in blue, green and brown, using lead, copper and magnesium oxides.

Tanneries were found mostly in Hebron and Jaffa. Here, in Hebron, are water skins made from a whole sheep's skin.
Below:
tanners scraping skins on the sea shore in Jaffa. In both towns, the tanners, like many other trades, had their own quarter.

16

17

The Growth of Large-scale Industry

In contrast to the slow but noticeable decline in small craft workshops during the Mandate, factory industry grew rapidly, concentrated mostly around Haifa, Tel Aviv and Jaffa. The largest enterprises were all in the Jewish sector: the monopolistic electricity concession given by the British to Pinhas Rutenberg, an engineer from Ukraine and a strong Zionist supporter; the Dead Sea potash works (another British concession won by Moses Novomeyski who formed the Palestine Potash Company, the major part (70%) of whose capital was from Jewish national sources – the Palestine Economic Corporation and the Jewish Colonial Trust); the Nesher Cement Company; the Shemen Oil Company; and the Atlit Salt Works. The capital invested in these enterprises, both from private Jewish sources and Zionist national funds, was substantial: the capital of the Palestine Electric Corporation which ran the Rutenberg concession was £P 1 million in 1930; Nesher's capital was £P 300,000 in 1927; Shemen's £P 169,000 in 1929; and the Palestine Potash Company's £P 250,000 in 1930.

On the Arab side, numbers of new enterprises, including factories, were established but capital mobilisation was not on a comparable scale. Where there was direct competition, as was the case in the soap and oil industries, the smaller, less capital-intensive, even if long-established local industry had a hard time surviving.

On the other hand, the gulf between Jewish and Arab industry can be exaggerated. The simple juxtaposition of, for instance, a photograph of the Nesher cement works against a small Arab workshop is somewhat misleading. First, there were larger Arab factories and second, up until World War II at least, much of Jewish industry was also on quite a small scale. Censuses of Jewish industry showed that the average number of employees per industrial enterprise was 14.9 persons in 1933 and 14.2 in 1937. This did not include what were defined as handicrafts where the numbers were 2.1 and 2.0 respectively. Nonetheless, even these smaller enterprises tended to be more capital-intensive, using, for example, electric power more often than hand or animal power.

18

Nesher Cement Works near Haifa (1948), one of the largest Jewish-owned factories in Palestine. It supplied a large portion of local building needs and benefited from protection imposed by the government in the form of a high tariff on imported cement. Unlike the Shemen Oil Company (see over) Nesher employed some Arabs as well as Jews, though only for unskilled work.

19

Diamond polishing, an example of a branch of Jewish industry which started on a small scale in 1938 but developed rapidly during World War II as a result of increased demand for industrial cutting diamonds. Skills for this industry came from Jewish immigrants from Belgium and Holland, formerly centres of the diamond-cutting industry.

Large foreign concerns, particularly British ones, also gained important sections of the Palestine market, both in industrial and consumer goods. Shell, in partnership with the Anglo Persian Oil Company, built a refinery in Haifa in 1939 to process oil from Iraq.

112

20

The soap industries of Nablus and Jaffa – again small-scale workshop production – nonetheless provided the most important manufactured export from Palestine in the nineteenth and early twentieth centuries. The soap was made from the pure olive oil favoured by Muslims, coming mostly from local groves and being processed with an alkali in a vat, as seen here. In 1927 there were 24 such factories in Nablus, employing an average of 5 to 6 workers each. Labour was hired on a contract basis by a ra'is or supervisor who also controlled production.

21

Soap being hand-wrapped in the factory of Ahmad Shaka'a in Nablus, whose brand name was Jamal *or* Camel. *The soap industry came to grief in the 1930s for two main reasons. First Egypt, which had previously provided a market for almost half the annual production of Nablus soap, followed a world-wide trend in the recession and raised high tariff barriers against imported soap to protect its own industries. Second, the possibility of selling the resulting surplus on the home market was diminished by the appearance of a competitor in the form of a large new Jewish-owned soap and oil factory in Haifa.*

22

Shemen Oil Industries was established in the 1920s with a capital of £E 250,000. It produced soap, olive and other oils, cattle cake and a variety of other products. In the 1930s its machine line-produced soaps were cheaper than Nablus soaps and thus contributed to the undermining of the latter's market. Shemen also succeeded in the late 1920s in persuading the government to lift duties on imported oils used in their soaps. Since the Nablus industry mainly used local olive oil (except when the harvest was very poor) this did little to help it, and the lifting of import duties on sesame oil was decidedly unhelpful for agriculturalists who grew sesame for export. In contrast, when the Palestine soap industry got into difficulties in the 1930s, the government did little to assist it.

Since ancient days Palestine has been known as the homeland of the olive, but only with the foundation of Shemen Works did her olive oil gain world-wide fame.

SHEMEN

Founded in 1922, Shemen Works stand out to-day as the biggest industrial enterprise of its kind in the whole Middle East, its superior olive oil & soaps reaching

68 COUNTRIES ALL OVER THE GLOBE

Tourists are cordially invited to visit the Shemen Factory in Haifa

THE WORLD KNOWN BRAND FROM THE HOLY LAND

BUY "SHEMEN" PRODUCTS.

REFINED SESAME OIL	Finest Table Oil
REFINED SUNFLOWER OIL	Best for Health
"KOKOSIN"	Best for cooking, Snow-White
REFINED OLIVE OIL	Highest Quality
BOILED LINSEED OIL	Quick Drying
MARSEILLE SOAP 72%	Extra Pure, Most Economical
OLIVE OIL SOAP	100% Olive Oil Nablus Quality

SHEMEN Ltd., HAIFA

LARGEST and MOST UP TO-DATE FACTORY in the NEAR EAST

The advertisement for Shemen soap here ironically promotes it as being of 'Nablus' quality, thus appropriating the virtues of its competitor. The other advertisement, aimed also at the export market, plays on the well-worn Holy Land theme and manages to link it with the advantages of modern capitalist industry.

115

23 24

A number of larger-scale Arab-owned factories were established in the 1920s and 1930s.
The main machine room of the Eastern Match Works Company in Nablus and one of the proprietors posed at his desk (1940).

116

25
Nazareth Arab Cigarette and Tobacco Company: women at work separating tobacco leaves for drying (1940). At this time it was still comparatively rare to use women as cheap unskilled labour in industrial enterprises.

26
Masri Company Flour Mills in Nablus (1940), one of the larger flour mills in the country, producing 40 tons of flour a day and working round the clock in three shifts — an unusual organisation of work in the Arab sector at this time.

The Building Industry

Population growth in the towns meant that the
building industry did a brisk trade and urban land
prices rose considerably. This trend began as early
as the 1880s and 1890s and continued, though with
some interruptions in times of war, rebellion and
depression, right through the Mandate. In the
long-established towns like Jerusalem, Jaffa and
Nablus wealthier families moved out of the old
city centres into handsome stone houses on the
outskirts. In Nablus, Jerusalem, Ramle and Lydda
a good deal of rebuilding had to be done after the
destruction caused by a serious earthquake in 1927.
Tel Aviv, of course, was almost entirely a
twentieth-century creation, and likewise Haifa,
where the small old town near the harbour was
gradually dwarfed by the new commercial centre
and housing which climbed up the slopes of
Mount Carmel.

27

Destruction in the centre of
Nablus caused by the
earthquake which struck
central Palestine on 11 July
1927. In all 272 people were
killed and 833 wounded in
Palestine and Transjordan.

118

*The stone mason at work on
the left seems somewhat
incidental to this picture. His
craft was revived by the
growth of building activity
from the 1880s onwards. It
was encouraged in Jerusalem
during the Mandate by a
British regulation that all
new buildings should be
stone-faced, which helped to
fend off the encroachments of
concrete and cement as the
main building materials.*
Below:
*the mason and overseer who
built St George's cathedral in
Jerusalem, with the symbols
of their trade.*

*Gunpowder makers at work
in a cave near Beit Jibrin,
south-west of Jerusalem.*
Below:
*preparing a blast. The
explosives were mostly used
in quarrying – a major
occupation in the nearby
Bethlehem area.*

31

32
Opposite:
*livestock market in the
Birket as-Sultan, Jerusalem,
around the turn of the
century. Towns remained
focal points for trade in
agricultural goods and
livestock for the peasants and
bedouin of the surrounding
areas.*

Commerce and Trade

During the Mandate commercial and service concerns proliferated in all the major towns. On the whole, the Jewish and Arab sectors directly overlapped only to a limited extent, though it seems that in the wholesale business, particularly in agricultural goods, Arab traders did sell to the Jewish market. For instance, the Jewish agricultural expert Dr. Arthur Ruppin told the Palestine Royal Commission that in 1935 'Arab farmers sold £P 500,000 worth of agricultural produce to Jews'. (Palestine Royal Commission, *Minutes of Evidence*, p. 107).

New enterprises started up to cater for the new tastes of a growing urban middle class, though this group remained too small for the market ever to reach mass proportions. There were, however, definite signs of its existence by the 1930s. A glance at the *Arab Commercial Directory* for 1937-8 reveals that consumer durables – gramophones, radios, records, watches – all with standard European brand names, were on sale in Haifa, Jaffa and Jerusalem. Fashion shops and hairdressers were also to be found. For most of the Palestinian population, even in the big towns, however, neither money nor taste admitted the adoption of such styles.

Basic foodstuffs were still mainly sold unpackaged and canned or processed products were not very common. However substantial amounts of most basic goods such as oil, flour, rice, kerosene, matches, tea, coffee, sugar and salt were imported and under the British were subject to heavy import duties which raised the price to the consumer.

Large-scale commercial activity continued to centre around trade, foreign and local, in agricultural goods where brokers and commission agents proliferated. Two new branches of trade flourished – one in response to demand for everything associated with building and another, rather later, with the motor trade, as the numbers of both commercial and private vehicles on the roads increased.

In the villages, more general stores were opened and there was a decline in the number of peddlers who had hawked agricultural and other sorts of goods around the villages. The 1931 census recorded that there were about 2,000 peddlers of whom 28 were women. However, the demand for their services diminished subsequently.

32

33

A melon market outside the Jaffa Gate, Jerusalem. Melons were a speciality of the Tulkarm area but were marketed all over the country and exported to Syria and Egypt.

34

Pottery for sale in a street in Ramle. Ramle was a small town sited on both the road and the railway route between Jerusalem and Jaffa and, like nearby Lydda, grew rapidly during the years after 1890, benefiting commercially from its strategic position.

122

35

Shopkeepers posing with their wares. Most of the groceries stocked here – which would include flour, sugar, spices, garlic, dried chillies (hanging up), rice and other grains – would be sold loose by weight. A few packaged goods can be seen on the shelves, however, along with paraffin lamps – a much-used form of lighting in homes with no electricity.

36

Cotton-filled quilts – a common kind of bedding, rolled up or folded away during the day. From the 1830s to the 1860s, Palestine had grown some cotton for export. A boom period of very high prices during the American Civil War in the early 1860s was followed, however, by a slump when Palestinian cotton could not compete in quality with that of Egypt. After World War I very little was grown and raw cotton as well as yarn was imported in increasing quantities.

37

37 38

Food selling: a stall selling
filafel, *fried balls of crushed*
chickpeas eaten as a snack
with bread and opposite *a*
sweetmeat shop with the
sweets displayed on large
trays.

38

39
The gramophone holds pride
of place in this café. Note also
the bottled drinks on sale.

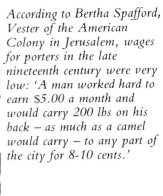

40

According to Bertha Spafford, Vester of the American Colony in Jerusalem, wages for porters in the late nineteenth century were very low: 'A man worked hard to earn $5.00 a month and would carry 200 lbs on his back – as much as a camel would carry – to any part of the city for 8-10 cents.'

41

A lemonade seller on a railway station platform.

42
Shoe blacks at the Jaffa Gate,
Jerusalem.

Wage Labourers

Two kinds of population drift were occuring simultaneously by the 1930s. The largely seasonal movement of people from the villages seeking employment in and around the towns has been mentioned, but this was combined with an influx of people to the cities from the smaller towns where employment opportunities were static or in decline. For instance, in 1934, unemployment was said to be serious among Arab workers in Nablus, Jenin, Tulkarm and in Jaffa, particularly among soap workers, building labourers, souvenir makers and orange box makers. Some of these people probably moved elsewhere in search of work.

Exact numbers of Arab wage labourers are impossible to come by because so much of the workforce was seasonal and fluctuating. However, it was estimated that in 1936 Jaffa port employed around 2,000 Arab workers, Haifa port fluctuated between 800–1,600, and the railways employed a total of about 3,000 Arabs by 1936. In the orange picking season, an estimated 8,000 Arabs worked in Jewish orange groves and up to 15,000 in Arab groves in the mid to late 1930s. Added to this were quite numerous short-term jobs on public works contracts.

The biggest of these was the construction from 1929 to 1933 of Haifa harbour. Here a clash of interests arose. The Public Works Department of the government wanted to hire low-paid, unskilled Arab workers for stone quarrying and construction to lower the costs of the project. The Jewish Agency and the Histadrut (the Jewish trade union organisation), on the other hand, pressed for the employment of more expensive Jewish unionised labour. This was also a bone of contention on road building projects, especially in the late 1920s when there was a recession in the Jewish sector of the economy and unemployment was high.

Some Jewish factories took Arab labour – though by no means all. This form of employment was thought to total about 1,500 in the first half of the 1930s. Arab-owned factories probably employed between 3,000–4,000.

Living conditions for those without a permanent home in the city were often makeshift. Rents by the 1930s were high and the inevitable result was the mushrooming of 'tin towns' in Haifa and Jaffa. By 1936 one local observer (George Mansur) estimated that about 11,000 people lived in Jaffa shanty towns and roughly as many again in Haifa, though undoubtedly the numbers depended on the time of year.

Wage rates in occupations employing Arabs and Jews in the 1930s:		
	Wages: (mils per day)	
Occupation	Arab	Jewish
Orange picker (1933)	80–100 (men)	200 (men)
Citrus plantation worker (1936)	150	175–200
Nesher Cement Works (1936)	165	320
Soap makers and workers in oil mills (1937)	250–550	350–480
Semi-skilled metal workers (1937)	150–200	200–400

(Collected from Government Annual Reports, Palestine Royal Commission Minutes of Evidence and S. B. Himadeh, *The Economic Organisation of Palestine*)

43

Porterage in Haifa Harbour. According to a government memo in January 1935, 'porterage for all goods except imported coal and exported citrus was under the control of Muhammad Kamil Namoura, appointed by the Director of Customs, who had in his regular employ 80 Arabs (the Jewish labourers who were formerly employed left some time ago, able to find higher rates of pay elsewhere) and between 600 and 700 casual daily labourers.' Citrus exports were handled by labourers hired directly by the exporters (from Public Record Office – Colonial Office Records).

HAIFA. Harbour, Embarking & disembarking.   חיפה, הנמל, פריקה וטעינה

128

44

Atlit stone quarries near Haifa, which provided much of the building material for the harbour. The quarries attracted a number of migrant labourers between 1929 and 1932: by September 1932 there were 379 Arab workers (87% of the total) and 55 Jewish workers (13%). The Public Works Department preferred cheaper Arab labour but under pressure from the Histadrut (Jewish trade union organisation) Jewish workers were put on piece work and were thus able to earn more than the Arab workers who were on a fixed daily wage.

45

Stone quarry on Mount Carmel owned by the Jewish construction company Solel Boneh, which has since become one of the largest construction concerns in Israel. It is owned by the Histadrut.

46

Jewish picket in 1934 outside Rapaport orange grove in Kfar Saba, part of the Histadrut's campaign for the exclusive employment of Jews in all Jewish owned establishments. The placard reads: 'Don't dispossess the Jewish worker.'

These migrant and semi-migrant workers might not have been all that significant in numerical terms, compared at least with the whole working population, but they were a new and marginal social group. Some still had strong roots in their villages but while they were in the cities they had no accepted social role or position compared, for instance, with shopkeepers or skilled craftsmen, however poor. They neither had the safety net of the charitable institutions on which at least some sections of the urban poor had previously been able to rely – they were too numerous for that – nor had they the benefit of cohesion and organisation pro-

vided by a strong trade union movement such as Jewish workers had.

The Histadrut was hostile to Arab workers being employed in any Jewish enterprise and mounted a strong campaign in the 1930s to enforce the concept of *avoda ivrit* (Hebrew labour) on Jewish employers. Their action, combined with the disruptive effects of the 1936 general strike and the subsequent rebellion, further separated the two sectors of the economy and increased the tension and hostility between the two communities, particularly in the main cities where contacts were less avoidable than in the countryside.

47

A storyteller and his audience in a poor quarter of Haifa, probably in the 1940s. The makeshift stage is made from boxes which carried construction materials from a company in London. In the audience, two men can be identified as porters – they are still wearing the padding which protected their backs and shoulders.

131

1
Coffee house in Jerusalem.
Only men would sit in such
places.

6 CHANGING LIFESTYLES

Using photographs to evoke lifestyles in the towns presents different kinds of problems to showing family and social life in villages. In towns, only parts of this life were conducted in the public gaze and there was a much stronger division between 'public' and 'private' life. Business and male socialising – in the coffee house, khan (inn) or shop – were quite accessible to the camera, but women are much less often seen. Those who are seen in the streets are frequently women from the villages come to market. The latter would seldom be seen veiled, whereas for women who lived in towns this was much commoner.

Architecture, particularly in old cities like Jerusalem, Jaffa, Hebron or Nablus, also conspired to keep prying eyes away from private life. Houses usually presented blank walls to the street with a small door leading into an enclosed courtyard where much of the home's life would go on invisible to those in the street. The newer style of handsome stone houses built by the wealthy on the outskirts of the towns was closer to that of Europe, but like European houses of the same status, they were often secluded by gardens or walls.

The first part of this chapter illustrates the kind of public social occasions, many related to religious celebrations, which were easily accessible to outside observers and their cameras. The second part enters briefly the realms of family life, which formed the centre of most people's social world. The examples collected here do not purport to be a socially or geographically representative sample. Only a relatively small section of society took or kept pictures of its own family histories. The photographs shown do not cover the whole spectrum of society which did commit its memories to film but gives some idea of how a few groups of families viewed themselves and how they evolved, socially and economically, over two to three generations.

2

A café on a balcony above a filafel *stall, Jerusalem.*

133

Jerusalem houses did not all
have their own water supply,
and many people had to
collect their water from the
neighbourhood water stand.
Above:
in the Old City (from
people's dress, this shot was
obviously taken in winter)
and
below:
outside the walls to the north
of the Damascus Gate near
the Nablus road.

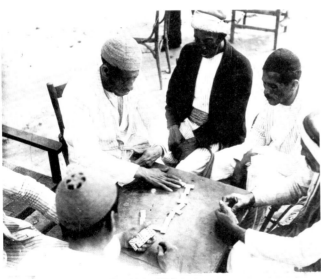

56

Above: *a Bonfils photo entitled 'Peasants playing tric-trac' (backgammon) in Jerusalem. The setting, however, is neither a café, nor outside a shop, where peasants visiting Jerusalem might be expected to go to play, drink coffee and smoke a nargileh (water pipe), but the yard of a house. This raises the question of whether the photographer has simply set up this scene for his own convenience.*
Below:
a game of dominoes, another popular pastime.

7

8

7 8

*A beggar woman and child in
Acre* (above) *and a blind
man begging in the Garden of
Gethsemane, Jerusalem*
(below). *It was generally
considered praiseworthy to
give alms to the poor and this
was institutionalised by
religious charities, both
Muslim and Christian.*

9
Friday food rations being distributed in Jerusalem by a charitable institution (Friday is the Muslim holiday).

10
Inmates of the Moravian Leper Hospital in Jerusalem in pre-World War I days. Diseases like leprosy were brought under control during the Mandate.

Lepers in the Moravian Leper Home at Jerusalem.

11

A pre-World War I Nebi Musa festival, with crowds outside the Old City waiting for the procession. Though women from the towns usually kept apart, especially during the 'camp-out' in Jericho, peasant and bedouin women mingled freely with their menfolk. For reasons obvious from this picture, Nebi Musa was also called the 'feast of the umbrellas'. It normally fell close to the Greek Orthodox Easter, a time of year when sunshine is often interspersed with rain. Merchants and peddlers, selling food, drink and trinkets, did a roaring trade during these days.

12

Nebi Musa (the Muslim festival of the prophet Moses) was a major annual event. Thousands of pilgrims came from the villages surrounding Jerusalem and from as far afield as Hebron and Nablus to march in procession from Jerusalem to the shrine of the prophet, south-west of Jericho near the Dead Sea, where they camped out and celebrated for several days. Here, prayers are held outside Jerusalem. The banners carried in the procession signified groups from different towns, villages or quarters of towns.

3522 Neby Mousa. Procession. Pèlerins s'arrêtant et Se Pélerinage pour Neby Mousa (La prière).

13
Nebi Musa, 1933: dancers accompanied by a long flute (nayeh). The well-to-do of Jerusalem sit on the stands. The feast directly involved the city's dignitaries: and the mayor was presented with the Nebi Musa banner at the beginning of the procession. The shrine itself was under the care of the Hussaini family of Jerusalem, one of whose members, Haj Amin Hussaini, was at this time Grand Mufti of Jerusalem. The procession was also frequently an occasion for political protest during the 1920s and 1930s.

14
Nebi Musa was only the most important of a number of such festivals around the country. Here is a circumcision procession during the festival of Nebi Rubin, celebrated by villagers in the area south of Jaffa. The boys to be circumcised are seated in the pannier on the camel.

15
Nebi Salih celebrated in Ramle in 1943. Note the changing styles of dress in contrast to the earlier Nebi Musa photographs.

16

The Greek Orthodox ceremony of the Washing of the Feet at the Holy Sepulchre Church in Jerusalem on Maundy Thursday, with the Patriarch of Jerusalem in attendance. The Greek Orthodox community was the largest Christian group in Palestine. During the late nineteenth and early twentieth centuries it went through considerable turmoil, as local Arab members of the church grew increasingly resentful of the domination of the Greek clergy. They demanded that Arabs should be allowed to rise in the ranks of the clergy and be eligible for the Patriarchate of Jerusalem. Before World War I they were supported in their claim by Russian Orthodoxy, which was attempting to gain a more secure foothold in Palestine.

17

17

Christmas day procession at the Church of the Nativity in Bethlehem. Added to the foreign pilgrims and tourists who came to the town for this occasion were people from villages around the Bethlehem area.

Haj Aref Qasim Abboushi of Jenin, who was born in 1869 and died at the age of 90 in 1959, a lifetime which saw three sets of rulers – Turks, British and Jordanians (Jenin is in what is now known as the West Bank, ruled by Jordan from 1948-1967). He was a large landowner and in Turkish times was also amin as–sunduq, *the town treasurer.*

19

The same family, two generations on, in a wedding photograph from 1942. The wife came from a merchant family in Jenin. Her mother was from Lebanon and her father's family came, some 100 years before, from Hebron. Note the western-style wedding dress — these fashions were often imported from Beirut.

20

The Abboushi family had strong links with Beirut, through business and education.
Below: members of the family in Beirut in the early 1920s. Most of the young men in this picture went to the American University there, except Fahmi Abboushi (far right, seated), who went to the French-speaking College of St Joseph, also in Beirut. Fahmi returned home and became mayor of Jenin from 1935 to 1937. A strong supporter of the nationalist movement, he was dismissed from office by the British in 1937 and returned to Beirut. Fa'iq Abboushi (seated, second from left) became a doctor and remained in Lebanon. With them are members of two other important families in the central area of Palestine: (standing, left) Muhammad Abdul Hadi: (seated, second from right) Salim al-Haj Ibrahim, from an important family in the Tulkarm area.

20

21

A member of the Palestine Police, Salih Azouka, being decorated in 1937 with a medal for 'gallant and distinguished service' during 1936 by the Inspector-General of Police and Prisons, R.G.B. Spicer. The Azouka family, one of the oldest in Jenin, had traditionally sent their sons to al-Azhar University for religious education. Salih, later Mayor of Jenin (1959-63), did not follow this tradition. After studying at the Muslim Salahiyya school in Jerusalem, he worked as a teacher before joining the police.

22

The professions — medicine, law and teaching — became increasingly attractive in the Mandate period when there were fewer openings than previously in the administration. However, the first generation of sons from well-to-do families who were sent off for higher education before World War I had usually been destined for government service. Ruhi Bey Abdul Hadi, shown here, who served under both the Turks and the British, received his BSc degree at Istanbul University and then entered the Turkish foreign service. Under the British Mandate he became an administrative officer in government service.

23

A qadi (Muslim judge in the shari'a – religious – courts) with his family. Judge Mutei Othman Darwish Ahmad al-Asir was born in Nablus in 1870. His father, a rich merchant, unlike the families above, did not believe in educating his sons, wanting them to work in his business. Mutei, however, having done very well at the kuttub, finally succeeded in raising the money to go to al-Azhar University in Cairo where he got a degree in Islamic law. He later went to Istanbul for further studies, taking with him his wife who also came from Nablus. He worked as a judge, first in Turkey and then in Syria (in Kunaitra, Homs and Hama), and later in Salt, at that time the largest town in what became Transjordan. During the Mandate he worked as a judge in Palestine (the shari'a courts remained independent of the British civil and criminal code) in Haifa, Jaffa, Jerusalem and finally Jenin, where he retired in 1926. Unlike his father, he favoured education – for his daughters as well as his sons. Two of his daughters became teachers (one later a headmistress); one son became a qadi and the other a doctor.

147

24

Families from different towns often had strong ties through business and intermarriage. Here members of several families (all Christian) from Jerusalem and Jaffa are gathered at the home of the Abdo family in Jerusalem (1922). The occasion was a party following the wedding of Abdulla Elias Abdulla to Julia Bardqash. Her father, from Jaffa, was a businessman who owned orange groves and a soap works. During World War I, the family were on good terms with the Turks, and were permitted to stay in Jaffa when it was evacuated by order of the Turks and many people were deported (see p 163). Abdulla's family, also from Jaffa, were less lucky, being deported to Anatolia for the rest of the war. This family also owned land, exported oranges and, in Turkish times, imported timber. They were connected by marriage to the Abdo family of Jerusalem, whose home this was. Several of the younger men of these families worked in the administration or in commerce. Andrea Abdo (far left, in tarbush) was the local representative for Singer sewing machines in Jaffa. Edmond Abdulla started out as an employee in Jaffa of Socony Vacuum of the USA, a major supplier of oil and fuel. George Mushabeq (a member of another family related to the Abdos) worked in the Customs Department. The Abdos had strong business ties with another family represented here – the Farraj family of Jerusalem. The firm of Farraj & Abdo, of Jaffa Road, Jerusalem, were general merchants selling building materials, ironmongery, oils and paints. In the centre of the back row is Yacoub Farraj, one-time deputy mayor of Jerusalem (the mayor was always a Muslim, his deputy Greek Orthodox) and a member of national political bodies – the Arab Executive and the Arab Higher Committee (see p. 170). He was one of those members of the Greek Orthodox community who campaigned for the 'arabization' of the church in Palestine. Before World War I he was honorary consul for Russia in Jerusalem and seems to have been something of a russophile. Russian names crop up quite frequently in this interconnected group of families. The one woman in the picture not wearing European dress is described in the arabic caption simply as fallaha, a peasant woman – probably a servant with the household.

(Some of the names used here are pseudonyms).

Two contrasting families from Ramalla, who became connected by marriage.

Above:

the Muhawi family, wearing traditional dress – in the case of the women, that characteristic of Ramalla. Ramalla was little more than a village until the Mandate period, but it gradually became a flourishing business community. An unusually large number of people from Ramalla emigrated before and during the Mandate, mostly to the USA where there is now a large Ramalla community. Those who were successful sent money home and this added to the town's prosperity. Mansur Muhawi, the old man in the centre of the picture, owned some agricultural land, olive groves outside Ramalla on the road to Tireh and had a shop in the nearby village of Beit Ur. His father had been a shoemaker in Nazareth who moved to Ramalla and married into one of its seven major families. He holds a large book although he was illiterate. His wife, seated, is Subha Salah. The daughter on the left, Khadra, became a businesswoman and sold fabrics. The son in the picture, wearing a tarbush, is Gerias, who became a doctor. His education was paid for by another brother who went to the USA. Another brother, Yusuf (not shown here) is said to have landed up in Wales just before World War I – probably he was trying to emigrate to the USA. He stayed in Wales for some time, selling oriental wares supplied from Palestine. Later he ran a travel agency (in Palestine) which specialised in travel to the USA. Yet another brother, Khalil, succeeded in extricating himself from military service three times (the family was Christian) but failed a fourth time and died in Turkey in 1917 or 1918.

Below:

the Audi family of Ramalla, urban landowners who owned Ramalla's largest hotel, the Grand Palace. They were Greek Orthodox until the late nineteenth century when they became Quakers. Wearing a tarbush on the right is Elias Audi. His wife Emily, seated next to him, came from Lebanon at the age of 16 and became a teacher in the Quaker school in Ramalla. The two younger daughters shown here, Ellen and Najla, both married members of Mansur Muhawi's family. Najla and the two sons in the picture, Salim and Aziz all emigrated. Three older sisters (not shown here) were sent to the USA just before World War I – through an immigration agency, supposedly to be educated, but when they arrived they found they were expected to work as maids. When the family realised that the agency had cheated them, they sent money for the girls to go to school. They stayed in the USA, and later they opened up two fashion shops together, one in Florida and the other in North Carolina.

25

26

Education was increasingly viewed as a means to social and economic mobility for poorer people and as a way of maintaining status for the better-off, as some of the older symbols of power and wealth were becoming eroded or insecure. Since 1948, this emphasis on education has been much further magnified among Palestinians by the lack of other forms of security and status.

Education for women began on a small scale around the turn of the century. The first school was established by the Quakers in Ramalla in 1889 (the boys' school followed in 1901). A Muslim girls'school was set up in Jerusalem soon after this. The 1931 census showed the highest proportion of literate Muslim and Christian women in the Jerusalem area where most of the opportunities for women's education were concentrated.

Most of the major private schools were run by missionaries or other religious bodies, Christian and Muslim, but the schools' intake was not on completely sectarian lines. For instance, many of Palestine's major Muslim families had their sons educated at the Anglican St George's School in Jerusalem, a prestigious establishment run on English public school lines. The British Mandate education department's initial ambitious plans to provide enough primary school places for all children quickly came to grief because their budget was far too small. This did not include Jewish children. Jewish schools became entirely separate because the Zionist Organisation insisted on Hebrew as a medium of instruction for all Jewish children. Since the British acquiesced in this, it was impossible to run an integrated school system. The following gives some idea of the paucity of government funding of education, bearing in mind that in 1946 Jews made up not more than 30% of the total population:

Figures in respect of education compare the amount expended annually on the maintenance of the Va'ad Leumi Jewish public school system (i.e. *excluding* the institutions of higher education and private Jewish schools) and the total expenditure of Government on the maintenance of Arab public system (i.e. *including* institutions of higher education but except for special grants not mission and private schools):–

	1933/34	1938/39	1943/44
Jewish public system	194,037	447,492	1,010,500
Arab public system	154,391	259,000	574,000

(*Survey of Palestine*, Vol II, p. 728.)

27

The fourth class at the Quaker Girls' School in Ramalla, December 1901, with their teacher, Najla Malouf.

28
Early picture of the Quaker Boys' School, also in Ramalla.

153

29 30

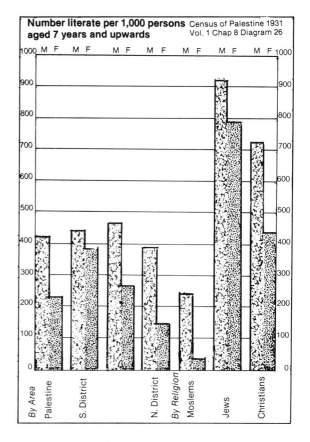

Number literate per 1,000 persons Census of Palestine 1931
aged 7 years and upwards Vol. 1 Chap 8 Diagram 26

*Six brothers from the
Hussaini family of
Jerusalem, all at St George's
Anglican school. Top left is
Jamal Hussaini, seen again
(below) in the light suit with
another old St George's
pupil, Izzat Tannous, on
one (probably 1936) of a
number of delegations to
London by Palestinian
leaders during the 1920s and
1930s to present their case to
the British government.*

30

31

Quaker group in Ramalla, including Katie Gabriel, the first headmistress of the Girls' School (second row from the rear, far left). Immediately to her right are Etta Johnson and Haldah Laighton, two American Quakers who were founder members of the school.

1

Kaiser Wilhelm II in Jerusalem, 1898, passing through one of several triumphal arches. The Emperor is on horseback preceded by the foreign consuls riding in carriages. Another of the arches carried a welcome inscription in Hebrew from Jerusalem's Jewish community. Theodor Herzl, one of the founders of Zionism, was at this time hoping to gain the Kaiser's support in persuading the Turkish Sultan to allow more Jewish colonisation. This picture was taken by a local photographer, Khalil Raad, and was published in a supplement to the Graphic *magazine in England in November 1898.*

Opposite: is an unflattering French view of the Kaiser's visit to Palestine, described as his 'divine mission'. It was part of a skit originally published in the French satirical magazine, Le Rire, *soon after the tour, and translated into English in 1918.*

2

Turkish soldiers drilling inside the Tower of David, Jaffa Gate, Jerusalem.

156

7 THE POLITICAL SCENE: WAR, POLITICS, RELIGION

Palestine's newsworthiness in the eyes of the world's media did not really begin until the upheavals of the late 1930s. Then, and in the period of virtual civil war after 1946, Britain's troubles in maintaining control of this semi-colony began to command headline status.

Before the 1930s, however, it only made 'hot news' on a few occasions. The first of these was in 1898 when Kaiser Wilhelm II of Germany visited Jerusalem. Ostensibly he went to open the Church of St John in the Old City, built on land given to his father by the Turkish Sultan, but his visit was also viewed by international opinion as a symbol of Germany's growing influence in the Ottoman Empire. It was also a festive and photogenic sort of occasion recorded by numerous local and foreign photographers, some of whom subsequently sold their photographs to the illustrated magazines of Europe.

An event of greater significance, for Palestine and for the world at large, was the British capture of Jerusalem in 1917. The glamour attached to the taking of 'the Holy City' was enhanced by the fact that it was part of a campaign subsequently roman-ticised for public consumption by T. E. Lawrence and the American journalist Lowell Thomas. Thomas's lectures on the Desert Revolt, illustrated by lantern slides and film, packed the Royal Opera House, Covent Garden, in 1919 and 1920. Their attraction was undoubtedly explained by the unmitigated grimness of almost every other theatre of that war but they also helped to reinforce the view in the British public that all Arabs were sword-brandishing warriors of the desert.

Probably more important in shaping the British public's view of Palestine than the wrangling and manoeuvrings at the Versailles Peace Conference where Palestine's future was decided, were the memories, descriptions and photographic souvenirs brought home by the British soldiers who had served in Palestine. Bertha Spafford Vester of the American Colony in Jerusalem, records that soldiers stationed there after 1917 were treated to lantern slide shows illustrating biblical sites in the 'Holy Land' they were busy occupying. Of these slides, the American Colony already had a large selection, thanks mainly to the photographic efforts of Eric Matson.

THESE PESTS, REPORTERS AND PHOTOGRAPHERS, ARE EVERYWHERE.

157

3
*Conscripts for the Ottoman
army marching northwards
out of Jerusalem in 1912 at
the time of the
Turkish-Bulgarian war.*

After the establishment of the Mandate there was a lull in media interest in Palestine until the mid-1930s, sporadically broken by reports of outbreaks of violence, and the visits of delegations and commissions of inquiry which usually followed closely upon such incidents. From 1936 to 1939 and from 1946 until the final British withdrawal from Palestine, the volume of news and pictorial coverage increased roughly in proportion to the intensity of conflict and violence. In a fashion not dissimilar to coverage over the years of events in Northern Ireland, newspaper readers were treated to an ever-increasing dosage of apparently meaningless violence – shattered buildings, dead and mutilated bodies, soldiers on guard, bomb-shocked civilians and so on.

Awareness of Palestine's problems among the public of Britain and other Western nations may have been confined to these dramatic symptoms but these nations had played a very considerable part in defining the shape of the problem. Whether or not this was recorded by newsmen and photographers, political decisions often made a good

many miles from Jerusalem, Jaffa or Nablus crucially affected the lives of Palestinians during this whole period, whether or not they actively responded to these changes.

The most radical and obvious change was the final disintegration of the Ottoman Empire during World War I which left this former province (or provinces) with new national boundaries and new rulers. Not that Ottoman rule had been universally popular in the Arab provinces of the Empire: the overthrow in 1908 of the corrupt regime of Sultan Abdul Hamid by the nationalist Young Turks (Committee of Union and Progress – CUP) was greeted at first with rejoicing in the Arab provinces. However, the 'turkification' policy of the CUP did not, as it turned out, leave much room for the specifically Arab nationalist aspirations which were growing in strength among the young and educated of Greater Syria (the area comprising what later became the mandated territories of Syria, Lebanon and Palestine). Another ingredient in the development of nationalist feeling which was specific to Palestine was Jewish colonisation which began in the 1880s. This did not go unnoticed among sections of the local population – notably peasants and bedouin who had been occupying land sold to the colonists by absentee landlords – and sporadic clashes with settlers occurred. Local notables in Jerusalem and elsewhere also lobbied Turkish officials and (after 1908) the Turkish Parliament for an end to this immigration, though without much practical effect. Prior to World War I, however, these issues touched a relatively small section of the population.

One particular feature of Ottoman rule which did have a widespread impact was conscription. Until 1908 this was compulsory for male members of the Muslim population, while Christians and Jews were normally exempted on payment of a special tax. Especially in the last years of the Empire, conscription was not just a matter of a year or two in the local barracks. Conditions were harsh, health hazards considerable and as a matter of policy conscripts were sent far from home. Yemen and the Balkans were possible destinations where nationalist or tribal uprisings against the Turks could not be put down with locally raised troops. Many people did not return from such expeditions.

World War I had a profound economic and political impact on Palestine and the disruption it caused affected most people's lives. This disruption did not just begin with the British invasion in 1917, for in previous years the Ottomans used Palestine as a base for attacks on the British in neighbouring Egypt. Conscription was extended to the whole male population including Christians and Jews – who were usually put to work in the labour corps under harsh conditions. Most attempts to avoid service during this time seemed to end in failure, though a few young men from influential families managed instead to do medical work.

4

Haj Mustafa Abboushi, a member of one of the main landowning families of Jenin, who lost an arm fighting in the Crimean War in Turkish service. This is a painting by a German, who was among the substantial number of Germans in Palestine during World War I assisting the Turkish war effort. The painting was done in Jenin in 1917, shortly before the Turks began to retreat northwards.

5

5

Olive tree being attacked by masses of locusts. During the 1915 plague of locusts, children from villages and Jewish settlements around Jaffa were taken out of school to collect locusts and their eggs, in an attempt to minimise the damage. The rewards offered – one metalik (about ½d at that time) for 5½ lbs of male locusts and a beshlik (about 6d) for the same amount of eggs – were very small considering how long it took to collect those quantities.

6 7 8

These photographs of the Gaza front in 1917 – seen from the Turkish side as they fought the British advance – were taken by Khalil Raad (see also no. 1). An official photographer with the Turkish army during the war, Raad had set up as a professional photographer with a shop in the Jaffa Road in Jerusalem in 1891. Late in the 1930s, it was still in existence, advertising itself as providing 'Artistic photography. Groups a speciality. Film developing and printing, cameras, photographs of the Holy Land.' 8 shows wounded soldiers in the Red Crescent hospital. The Red Crescent is the Muslim version of the Red Cross.

6

7

8

9

10

11

9 10 11

Snapshots taken by another Palestinian, George Elias Cassis (who appears in his shirt tails in the photograph on the above right) while working at a British relief camp in Al Arish (Sinai) in 1916-17 (no. 9). Along with a number of others who worked in this camp, he was a former pupil of the English St George's School in Jerusalem who had refused to serve in the Turkish Army against the British. Others, like the future nationalist leader Jamal Hussaini, seen on the left in no. 11 as a prisoner of war of the British in 1917, had worked in Red Crescent hospitals rather than serve in the army.

161

12
*'Big' Jamal Pasha,
Commander-in-Chief of the
Turkish Fourth Army,
reviewing troops outside
Jerusalem railway station,
1917. A year before he had
been responsible for the
execution of dozens of Arab
nationalists including several
Palestinians for belonging to
groups considered treasonable
by the Turkish authorities.*
Below:
*the title page of the book in
which appears the
correspondence said to have
been taken by the Turks from
French consulates in Beirut
and Damascus, incriminating
various Arab nationalists.*

13
*Hafiz Pasha Abdul Hadi of Jenin, a member of an important
family of landowners in Nablus, Arraba and Jenin. Hafiz
Pasha was a tax collector in Turkish times. His brother,
Salim Ahmad Abdul Hadi, a member of the Decentralisation
Party which demanded autonomy for the Arab provinces of the
Empire (founded 1912), was executed in 1916. Right is an
extract from* La Verité. . . *recording the verdict. The 'letter'
mentioned refers to Salim as the Jenin representative of the
party. Another member of the Abdul Hadi family, Awni
Abdul Hadi, was a founding member of the Arab nationalist
secret society Al Fatat, which he and six other Syrians and
Palestinians established in Paris in 1911, while pursuing
higher studies there.*

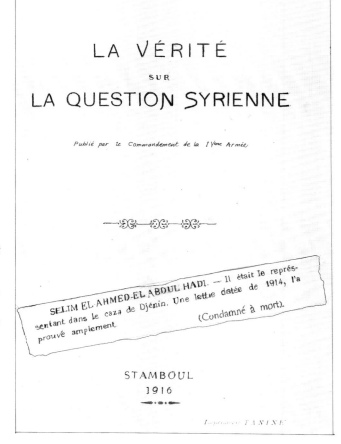

LA VÉRITÉ

SUR

LA QUESTION SYRIENNE

Publié par le Commandement de la IVème Armée

SELIM EL-AHMED-EL ABDUL HADI. — Il était le représ-
sentant dans le caza de Djénin. Une lettre datée de 1914, l'a
prouvé amplement (Condamné à mort).

STAMBOUL
1916

Imprimerie TANINE

162

According to the Nablus historian Ihsan Nimr, the Ottoman army requisitioned food supplies and fuel, creating shortages and consequently a black market and high prices. He added that in the Nablus area people – even in the towns – were reverting to olive and sesame oil for lighting when kerosene supplies ran out and bread was made out of barley, durra (sorghum) and bran instead of wheat. The value of paper money put out by the Turks declined by about 10% against gold and silver, not much by present standards but enough in a country unaccustomed to paper money to cause hoarding of goods and of gold.

The shortage of coal for the vital railway links led the Turks to chop down trees for fuel at random. In an area where there were few enough trees anyway this was a very serious loss. To add to the problems, a plague of locusts, (which periodically descended on Palestine) in 1915 ruined crops and trees.

The constant movement of troops to the south of Palestine, centre of the fighting until 1917, spread malaria, typhus and cholera epidemics. Once the British invasion began, cultivation ceased in areas in the path of the warring armies and villagers fled their homes until the danger passed. The population of Jaffa suffered an upheaval when the Turks ordered the town to be evacuated in 1917 as the British began their advance northward. Many people went to Jerusalem or Nablus, though some ended up as far afield as Homs or Hama in Syria. Only a few orange grove owners were permitted to stay to look after their property.

Turkish suspicions that some people among their subject Arab populations were actively interested in hastening the end of their rule were fired in 1915 by the discovery in French consulates in Syria of documents which named members of secret Arab nationalist societies. Among those nationalists summarily executed as traitors during 1915 and 1916 were several Palestinians. A certain number of important families from Jaffa were also deported to Anatolia in 1916 for the duration of the war, apparently because the German Consul had denounced them for 'entertaining sympathies' for the Entente powers.

Relief in 1918 that the war had ended gave way rather quickly to misgivings about Palestine's future under British rule. The shape of the Mandate gradually emerged from the fog of promises which wartime expediency had prompted the British to make to various incompatible national groups in the Middle East. A surge of militancy followed the collapse of hopes in 1920 of an independent Greater Syria under Britain's erstwhile protégé Amir Faisal from the Hijaz (western Arabia). It was helped along by the openness and, on occasion, arrogance with which the Zionists in Palestine expressed their aim for the rapid colonisation of the country. By the time the first High Commissioner, Sir Herbert Samuel, arrived in 1920, the shape of future battle lines was already emerging.

The British not only replaced the Ottomans as imperial overlords but introduced under their protection a largely European settler minority whose numbers, it was agreed under the Balfour Declaration and the League of Nations Mandate, would grow to the 'economic absorptive capacity' of the country. What this capacity precisely was remained a cause for debate among Zionists, British and Palestinians throughout the Mandate.

14

An unlikely beginning to British rule in Palestine. Jerusalem's mayor, Hussain Effendi al-Hussaini (centre, with tarbush, cane and cigarette) making a token surrender of the city to two British sergeants of the 219th Battalion, London Regiment, 9 December 1917.

163

From 1920 onwards, Palestinian political life was dominated by the question of how to react to the new rulers and their protégés, over whose arrival the local inhabitants had no control. That did not mean that everyone in the country had been perfectly content with Ottoman rule – far from it. It was precisely from the feelings of nationalism generated in opposition to Turkish rule in the Arab provinces that hopes of independence had grown up, only to be dashed by the early 1920s.

It was, in fact, the economic rather than the strictly political aspects of Zionism which, over time, built up fear of and hostility towards it among wider sections of the Palestinian population. The economic impact of this colonisation varied, depending on which section of the population one looks at. Landowners were obviously tempted by the high prices offered by Jewish land-buying agencies to sell land in order to acquire liquid capital for investment in other projects – or simply for speculation, according to taste. Peasants who owned land seldom sold it unless they were too much in debt to do otherwise, but for those who were tenants, there was the prospect of losing access to their land. The fear that this *might* happen, as much as the actuality, was a source of both anger and insecurity, especially in areas known to be prime targets for settlement.

Palestinian merchants and businessmen felt competition from the Jewish commercial sector, particularly in the expanding market for European consumer goods. In industry, the knowledge that there was a more or less constant flow of capital for investment from Europe contributed to the sense of many local entrepreneurs that it was difficult to compete in a comparatively unfamiliar and high-risk area of economic activity. There was also a growing feeling that the British concept of facilitating the Jewish National Home was not merely allowing the Zionists control of crucial economic resources like land, mineral sources and power (the British gave various Zionists and Zionist-controlled bodies several concessions on State lands as well as concessions to build a power station on the Yarmouk River and to exploit Dead Sea potash). Britain, it was believed, was also favouring Jewish enterprises with tariff concessions and creating work for Jewish immigrants when there was a shortage of work for Palestinians. Despite the constant complaints of the Jewish Agency that the British were insufficiently co-operative, primarily

over the question of how many immigrants should be let in at a time, Palestinians saw a rather different picture – in which the National Home had a status which fundamentally overrode whatever needs the Palestinian population might claim to have. In this context began the questioning of whether it would ever be possible to end the features of the National Home policy to which Palestinians objected without first getting rid of the British.

There was considerable popular feeling, from early in the Mandate period, against the terms under which Jewish immigration to Palestine was conducted. However, the feeling took a variety of forms according to social, economic and even educational factors. On the whole, what class or social group a person belonged to would also affect what, if anything, he was likely to do to express this opposition.

تمثيل

فتيان سورية الجنوبية

تمثل فرقة الكشافة العربية لمدرسة روضة المعارف رواية «انتصار العرب على العجم» أو «يوم ذي قار» تحت رعاية سمو الأمير فيصل ايده الله في الساعة التاسعة زوالية من ليلة الخميس المصادف ٢-٣ تموز سنة ٩١٩ في مسرح المدرسة الحربية ويدخل الفصول الحان موسيقية واناشيد وطنية نرجو تشريفكم في الوقت المعين

هيئة ادارة مدرسة روضة المعارف القدسية

'Presentation by the youth of Southern Syria.
The Arab scout group of Rawdat Maaref School present a play Victory of the Arabs over the Persians *or* The Day of Dhiqar *under the patronage of His Highness Amir Faisal (may God support him) at 9 o'clock in the evening on Thursday 2/3 July 1919 in the theatre of the military school. The performance will include music and national songs. We hope you will honour us by coming at the right (or appointed) time.*
Administration of the Rawdat Maaref School, Jerusalem'

Ticket to a play which, though it has a historical setting, is clearly nationalist in sentiment. The reference to Palestine as 'Southern Syria' and the dedication to Amir Faisal indicate the presenters' sympathies with his short-lived regime in Damascus which the French terminated the following year. Rawdat Maaref School was a private Muslim institution.

164

Forms of protest: An English edition of the Jaffa Arabic bi-weekly paper Filastin *protesting at the visit to Palestine of the author of the Balfour Declaration. The paper's owner, Issa Dawoud al-Issa, was a Christian, and may have felt the biblical text appropriate when addressing an English audience.*

Prop. and Responsible Editor

I. D. Elissa

Jaffa

P. O. B   194

Tel No   94

صاحب الجريدة
ومديرها المسؤول
عيسى داود العيسى
يافا

صندوق البريد   ١٩٤
التلفون   ٩٤

فلسطين

La Palestine

Jaffa, March 25th, 1925.   ✦ Wednesday ٢٥ اذار

يافا يـ ٢٥ اذار سنة ١٩٢٥

A Special Edition in English issued on the occasion of the visit to Palestine of LORD BALFOUR, the statesman with whose name is associated the Declaration which to the Arabs signifies the death knell of all the hopes they cherished when the victorious British Armies entered their country in 1918

" FOR WE WRESTLE NOT AGAINST FLESH AND BLOOD, BUT AGAINST PRINCIPALITIES AND POWERS, AGAINST THE RULERS OF THE DARKNESS OF THIS WORLD, AGAINST SPIRITUAL WICKEDNESS IN HIGH PLACES".
Ephesians VI 12.

16

15 16
Black drapery and black flags on buildings were another way of registering political dissent.

15

17

Relatively low levels of literacy did not prevent newspapers becoming an influential source of news and views. They were often read out loud in coffeeshops and at gatherings such as this.

18

Dawoud al-Issa (in grey suit), correspondent for Filastin *and son of the owner, in Amman, Transjordan, in 1935.* Filastin *and al-Karmil in Haifa were among Palestine's earliest Arabic newspapers, both established before World War I and both from that time on vocal opponents of Zionism, in which they were later joined by a number of other papers in the 1920s and 1930s.*

19

Most shopkeepers in Jerusalem keep their doors closed on the day of Lord Balfour's arrival in Palestine (March 1925). Members of the Palestine Police stand in the foregound.

VEILED ARAB WOMEN who waited on the High Commissioner at Haifa to present petitions concerning the riots. They were received by Mr. Perowne, Press Officer (left).

20
*Women, some veiled,
presenting a petition to the
High Commissioner in Haifa
during the 1933 riots.*

Among those to whom the populace at large looked for leadership until at least the 1930s were many 'notables' – landowners, merchants and ex- or present government officials – who relied mostly on diplomacy to achieve their ends, much as they had done in Turkish times. They petitioned British officials, sent delegations to London and, where they could, manipulated long-standing family and social ties to win allies and mobilise popular support. There were also others among this nationalist leadership who maintained that the balance of power was such that diplomacy and persuasion could never succeed. They looked instead to forms of mass mobilisation, peaceable or otherwise. This could be achieved from above through the existing leadership which could enlist the support of those who were beholden by patronage or other ties. Alternatively, the initiative could come from groups outside the established leadership.

21
*Christian Palestinian women
wearing European clothes
with the addition of the black
headscarf which was a symbol
of allegiance to the nationalist
movement. Taken in 1930s
or 1940s on a Jerusalem
rooftop with a panorama of
the Old City as a backdrop,
this view shows the Dome of
the Rock to the left with
al-Aqsa mosque – the smaller
dome – on the right.*

167

At the beginning of the Mandate few organisations existed which could mobilise people on grounds other than family ties or patronage, but slowly, during the 1920s and 1930s, new forms of association emerged. Young people at school (as today in the West Bank and Gaza) began to play a part in political activity, much to the dismay of the British in the education department. Teachers were also frequently among the more politically active and radical members of the community. During the 1936 General Strike many schools closed down because their pupils as well as teachers went on strike, demonstrated and picketed.

Another form of youth organisation was based on religious affiliation. There was a Young Men's Christian Association and a Young Men's Muslim Association in addition to clubs under the aegis of the Greek Orthodox Church. All of these became the focus of political debate and activity, especially in the 1930s, and often signalled discontent not only with Zionism or the British but with the more conservative of their elders. Various scout groups served a similar purpose and in the 1930s scouts were found even to be patrolling Palestine's beaches on the lookout for the growing numbers of illegal Jewish immigrants. By the 1930s, then, most teenagers (male and some female), growing up in towns especially, found political discussion, if not activism, hard to avoid.

Women were certainly not *expected* to be involved in political life but the Mandate period did see some development in the public role of women. It began with the establishment of women's clubs from 1919 onwards. The members tended to come from the urban middle and upper classes, Muslim and Christian, and certainly the leading lights of these organisations were mostly the wives and relatives of prominent political figures. Much of their work revolved around charitable activities and their role generally resembled that of women in the Egyptian feminist movement in the 1920s. Certainly, Palestinian women followed them in assuming that nationalism took precedence over demands they might make as women. The first congress of Palestinian women held in 1929 submitted the following demands to the High Commissioner:

We, the Arab women of Palestine, having been faced with great economic and political difficulties and seeing that our cause has not so far received the sympathy and assistance of which it is worthy, have finally decided to support our men in this cause, leaving aside all other duties and tasks in which we have hitherto engaged ourselves.

This deputation of all the Arab women in Palestine has now come to lay before Your Excellency their protests and resolutions passed in their first Congress and to ask, as of right, that our demands be granted.

The following is a brief summary of the resolutions of the Congress:

(i) To protest against the Balfour Declaration, which has been the sole cause of all the troubles that took place in the country, and which may arise in future. We consider that this country will never enjoy peace and tranquillity so long as this Declaration is in force.

(ii) To protest against Zionist immigration in view of the political and economic situation of the country.

(iii) To protest against the enforcement of the Collective Punishment Ordinance.

(iv) To protest against the maltreatment by the police of Arab prisoners.

(M.E.T. Mogannam, *The Arab Woman*, London, 1937, pp. 74-5.)

Until 1936 protests in the countryside against Jewish settlements by peasants or bedouin usually took the form of attacks on individual colonists and sometimes the burning of colonies' trees and crops. The strongest sources of grievance were loss of land or the threat of it and exclusion from employment by Jewish labour organisations. During country-wide outbreaks of violence as in 1920-1, 1929, 1933 and from 1936 to 1939 attacks on settlements were common. Often mutual reprisals between the parties would lead to further bloodshed. In the towns, an instant and widely employed expression of political disgust was the commercial strike, still a common method of protest in the West Bank and Gaza today. This did not, however, imply that shopkeepers were well organised politically. There were Chambers of Commerce in the major towns which certainly took a part in deciding on strike action (or otherwise) in 1936. However, these were on the whole not political bodies and similarly neither were the craft and professional associations to be found in most towns.

22

23

Another style of headdress symbolic of nationalism which has survived to this day is the kuffir, a cotton headcovering of white (or black and white squared) cotton held in place with a head rope. Originally it was worn by bedouin and sometimes by peasants, while the tarbush was city-wear. The kuffir was widely adopted in the towns during the 1937-8 rebellion to make it harder for the authorities to pick out the rebels – who came mostly from the countryside and wore kuffirs. Matson comments that there is 'not a tarbush in sight' in his photograph of Friday prayers at the al-Aqsa mosque in Jerusalem on 16 September 1938. On 17 October the rebels briefly gained complete control of the Old City before their final defeat by the British military.

23

22 24
Friday prayers in the mosque of a small town, Majdal, in the south. In 22 the shaikh preaches the sermon.

24

169

25

Members of the Arab Higher Committee, established in 1936 to co-ordinate the activities of various nationalist parties. Front row, left to right: Ragheb Nashashibi, chairman of the Defence Party; Haj Amin Hussaini, Grand Mufti of Jerusalem and president of the Committee; Ahmad Hilmi Pasha, general manager of the Arab Bank in Jerusalem (this bank, founded in 1930 with a capital of £P15,000 is now one of the major banks in the Arab world); Abdul Latif Salih, chairman of the Arab National Party; Alfred Rock, influential landowner. Back row, left to right: Jamal Hussaini, chairman of the Arab Party and leader of the Arab commission to London; Dr Hussain Khaldi, mayor of Jerusalem; Ya'cub Ghussain, president of the Arab Youth Committee; Fuad Saba, secretary of the Arab Higher Committee.

Despite the increasing size of the Palestinian wage-labour force in towns like Jaffa and Haifa by the 1930s, trade unions did not become a very important political or economic force. Until the 1930s they were mostly 'paper' organisations, though by 1943 they had increased in strength and membership had grown to an estimated total of more than 10,000. The comparative ineffectiveness of Palestinian trade unions was in marked contrast to the power of the exclusively Jewish trade union movement (the Histadrut) which organised a large proportion of the Jewish workforce. Palestinian trade unions laboured under particular difficulties, the greatest of which was the nature of the workforce. The great majority were unskilled migrant labourers from the countryside, often only working for wages during the slack season in agriculture. They were thus difficult to organise, for political or economic purposes, and were in any case quite unaccustomed to the notion of trade union activity. Such labour activity as there was, however, contributed to the mosaic of political clubs and organisations which sprang up in the main towns in the 1920s and 1930s. The most widespread of these in the 1920s were the Muslim-Christian associations which were formed after World War I to present a united front against Zionism. By the 1930s they had mostly become so faction-ridden as to be ineffective and other organisations took their place.

A more potent political influence among the growing numbers of urban poor was a small but significant movement which grew up around a Muslim religious preacher, Shaikh Izzadin al-Qassim, who became a popular leader in Haifa and the surrounding villages in the early 1930s. Born in Syria, he moved to Palestine after the French occupation in 1920 and established himself as a noted preacher in the mosques in the Haifa area and further afield in villages of Galilee and the Jenin region. He campaigned in strongly religious terms against Zionism but at the same time differed from other nationalist leaders in addressing his message mainly to the poor and dispossessed. He advocated organised violent action rather than the anarchic attacks which had characterised, for instance, the massacre of Jews in Hebron in 1929. He set up small clandestine groups to prepare the way for a wider rebellion, and these guerrilla bands carried out assassinations in the early 1930s. Shaikh Qassim himself was killed in 1935 in a clash with British forces in the Jenin hills. His death made him something of a national martyr and his guerrilla groups, though small, foreshadowed both in style and social composition those who took to the hills in 1936 and again in 1937-8.

The Rebellions

For the first decade of British rule, the majority of those who voiced grievances against Zionist colonisation still looked to the British, as rulers, to rectify them. In the 1930s, however, there was a gradual but decisive switch of viewpoint as it became clear that in fundamental respects the British were not prepared to make changes in the terms of the Mandate. Even the more cautious of the nationalist leaders could not but be influenced as the tide of hostility turned against the British. It was this hostility and frustration which culminated in the 1936 General Strike and the rebellion of 1937-8, following the announcement of the Royal Commission's plan for the partition of Palestine.

While there are differing views on precisely whom and what the strike and rebellion represented, there is no doubt that both were radically different from most previous sorts of protest. Both town and countryside were involved to an unprecedented degree as the six month urban-based strike in 1936 was paralleled by guerrilla activity in the rural areas. In 1937-8 the centre of resistance shifted to the rebels based in the hills. They made considerable tracts of country virtually inaccessible for the British and from their rural bases sporadically deprived both the British and local notables

of control in the towns. Even the Old City of Jerusalem was briefly occupied by the rebels in 1938.

Although the guerrilla bands undoubtedly put pressure for assistance on village people there is considerable evidence that numbers of peasants willingly took to the hills. What is more, in its later stages, the rebellion demonstrated the resentment of those who participated in it against *mukhtars*, village and urban leaders, Palestine police and anyone else who had collaborated with the British.

The rebels' main weakness, however, was that while they attacked all those – Zionists, British and local leaders – on whom social as well as political injustices were blamed – their action was almost exclusively military, their organisation was fragmented and they had no coherent social or political programme which could sustain them once the fighting was over. As it was, the rebellion was finally crushed by British military forces and little but exhaustion, demoralisation and memories – some heroic, some bitter – were left behind. The political nationalist movement was in flux – its influence over popular feeling had diminished and its leadership was scattered by voluntary exile or deportation by the British.

الانتداب بعد ١٩ سنة

After 19 Years of British Mandate

اللنبي في القدس سنة ١٩١٧

Allenby in Jerusalem – 1917

واكهوب في القدس سنة ١٩٣٦

Wauchope in Jerusalem – 1936

Cartoon (from a compendium of material translated from Filastin *in 1936) illustrating the changing attitude of Palestinians towards the British, from the high hopes of 1917 when General Allenby is welcomed by Jerusalem notables and populace to the repressive image of British authority in 1936, with High Commissioner Sir Arthur Wauchope, having discarded his 'civil' topper and cane, riding on a tank in a show of military force.*

26 27 28

Riots in Jaffa, 1933. This confrontation with the police, which left 26 dead and 60 wounded, is often considered the turning point in nationalist protest against Zionism, as it marked the switch of emphasis from direct attacks on Jews to confrontation with the British authorities. This incident occurred after police had refused to allow a thousand-strong demonstration to march from its meeting place near the town's main mosque. Demonstrators, some armed with sticks and stones, tried to break through the cordon, whereupon the police opened fire.

Below:
Jerusalem courtroom during the trial of leaders accused of organising the demonstration (13 October 1933). Left to right: Jamal Hussaini, Edmond Rock (seated) and Shaikh Abd al-Qadir al-Muzaffar. All signed bail against good behaviour except Muzaffar, who preferred six months in jail.

Front page lead in the Jerusalem daily Palestine Post *on 8 November 1936.*

PALESTINE MARTIAL LAW ORDER ISSUED

PROCLAMATION TO FOLLOW

20 Arab Casualties In Jaba Battle

THREE BRITISH WOUNDED

An officer and a private of the Dorsetshire Regiment and a private of the Lincolnshire regiment were wounded in an engagement near Jaba, southwest of Jenin. which lasted throughout yesterday afternoon until dusk.

Detachments from four battalions engaged in a converging movement upon a band whose presence had been reported earlier.

The battalions were the Dorsets, the Lincolns, the Royal Scot Fusiliers and the Beds and Herts, besides aeroplanes and armoured cars.

It is believed that 20 Arab casualties were inflicted by the

Definite Date Not Yet Set

(Reuter)

LONDON, Tuesday.— An Order-in-Council entitled "Palestine Martial Law Order" was issued in tonight's London Gazette.

The Order empowers the High Commissioner to delegate to the General Officer Commanding the Forces powers to make regulations for securing public safety and defence in Palestine.

The new Order will be brought into force by a Proclamation in Palestine, to be promulgated probably, tomorrow.

Later, the High Commissioner will decide, in consultation with Lieut.-General Dill, the Commander-in-Chief, when to issue a further proclamation delegating to General Dill the widest possible powers.

These powers will include the establishment of Military Courts and regulations which cannot be challenged by the ordinary Civil Courts.

Other provisions are for press censorship, arrests and deportations, control of harbours, control of transportation by land, air and water, control of trade and commerce, the infliction of communal fines, and the forfeiture or destruction of property as a punitive measure.

"STATUTORY MARTIAL LAW"

Although the Order, as Reuter says, may be brought into force today it is not likely that any definite steps will be taken immediately (writes a Political Correspondent.)

The law will need considerable discussion between the military and the civil authorities and much drafting of regulations.

It is true that preparations have long been made for Martial Law, but it is gathered that what is at present contemplated is not martial law as such but something approaching what experts call "Statutory Martial Law," Lieutenant-General Dill probably dealing with the situation by means of the wide powers to be delegated to him by the High Commissioner.

powers will eventually assume, it is not intended that there should be any general superceding of the civil by the military authority. The civil administration would continue to operate as at present except in so far as it concerns the departments whose activities are closely connected with those of the Army, such as communications, and public security.

(Continued on page 6, Col. 3.)

29

Armoured patrol in the streets of Jaffa, 1936.

30

30

Some of the leaders of the rebellion in the rural areas during the 1936 General Strike. Right to left: *Halim Bey Jasim (Iraq); Fakhri Bey Abdul Hadi; Fawzi Qawakji; Hamad Bey Saab al-Druze; two unnamed Iraqis. The rebellion was given a pan-Arab flavour by the arrival in August 1936 of a group of about two hundred volunteers from Transjordan, Syria and Iraq (including a Druze contingent). They were headed by Fawzi Qawakji, a former Ottoman army officer from Syria who had fought in the Syrian Druze rebellion against the French in 1925. He later joined the Iraqi army but resigned in 1936. The others in the photograph belong to the Iraqi and Druze contingents, with the exception of Fakhri Bey Abdul Hadi, a Palestinian who was second in command to Qawakji who, briefly, till the end of 1936, took overall command of the rebels' operations.*

174

31
Fawzi Qawakji

32

33

Sabotaged railway line at 'kilo 107' between al-Tireh and Lydda, 1936, one of numerous acts of sabotage against railways, electricity lines and the oil pipeline from Mosul in Iraq to Haifa during both the 1936 and 1937-8 rebellions.

34

Jenin – the market town whose hinterland was one of the main centres of the 1937-8 rebellion – under 22-hour curfew in May 1938.

35

Photograph allegedly found on the body of a guerrilla leader – probably Ibrahim Amouri – who was killed by a British military patrol on 9 November 1938 in his home village of Irtah in Nablus subdistrict. During the second phase of the rebellion, locally recruited guerrillas were more numerous. The social composition of these groups (or 'gangs' as the British called them) was mixed. Peasants probably formed the majority, along with bedouin (mostly from Galilee and the Nablus area), members of notable families both rural and urban and a scattering of escaped convicts.

36 37
*Punitive demolitions of
property and collective
punishments were part of
British policy. These
photographs of punitive
demolitions in the villages of
Aquir and Saqiya (Ramle
subdistrict) were taken in
1936 by James Pollock, an
administrative officer in the
Palestine government
(1930-9). He labelled them
the Aquir and Saqiya 'bangs'
(apparently the euphemism
used to describe demolitions).*

38
*Checkpoints, searches and
restrictions on movement
became a regular feature of
life during the rebellion. Here
police search an Arab bus on
the Jerusalem-Jaffa road.*

39

Inhabitants of Hebron being collected for search and questioning after a rebel raid on Barclays Bank DCO (19 August 1938). MacGillivray (see p. 72) records in his diary that a 'large gang penetrated Hebron and occupied the Police Station, the Post Office and Barclays Bank and stole rifles. Destroyed at least two buildings. Black Watch sent from Jerusalem to restore order, but [much of] the male population of Hebron evacuated and joined the band [ie guerrillas].'

40

Jewish colonists trying to put out a fire started by Arabs on the Plain of Esdraelon, September 1936. Attacks of this kind continued, but most Arab hostility was directed against the British and against other Arabs who were seen as collaborators with the British or the Zionists. During this period, however, there was a substantial build-up of Jewish defence units.

World War II

Politically, World War II was a lull before yet another storm. The Palestinians were partly placated when the British issued the 1939 White Paper following separate talks in London with Palestinian and Zionist leaders. It imposed a ceiling of 75,000 on Jewish immigration over the following five years and restricted the areas in which Jewish land purchases could be made. The Zionists reacted angrily but after the outbreak of war reluctantly abandoned disruptive action inside Palestine on the grounds that it was obviously more important to fight Hitler at that point than the British. Nonetheless, campaigning against the White Paper continued elsewhere, especially in the US, and the military strength and preparedness of the Haganah and other armed groups continued to grow. For the duration of the war, however, there was comparative peace in Palestine and, rather surprisingly, a general growth in economic prosperity.

Just as Palestine's vulnerability to fluctuations in the condition of the world's commodity markets had been obvious in the 1930s, so the effects of shutting off these pressures were felt during the early 1940s. The Axis blockade of the Mediterranean and the imposition of import controls on a wide range of agricultural and manufactured goods caused prices to rise rapidly, much to the benefit of local producers. Added to this was the concurrent expansion of the domestic market as large numbers of troops were stationed in Palestine. More jobs, mostly unskilled, became available in army camps and other government services, many of which were located not in major urban areas but out in the countryside.

41

Attempts were made by the British after the rebellion to rebuild their relations with the rural areas, in many of which they had completely lost control during 1938. Sir Harold MacMichael, the High Commissioner (in hat and dark glasses) is treated to hospitality by village notables (1939 or 1940).

42

Arab recruits to the British army during World War II marching in Nablus (6 May 1941). Recruitment was on a voluntary basis. In all, 9,000 Arabs signed up in various branches of the services. The presence of large British army camps scattered around the country provided work for many more.

The combination of high prices and more jobs in fact gave most benefit to the rural economy, much in need of a boost after the disruptions of the rebellion. Farmers could sell their crops – particularly olives, wheat, vegetables and fruit – at high prices but were not as completely dependent on the purchase of high-priced food and other commodities for their own subsistence as were people living in towns. At the same time, more jobs and better wages were available to supplement agricultural income. Some observers maintained the war period did a great deal to diminish and sometimes even wipe out the chronic indebtedness which had been a constant feature of peasant life until that time. Poorer people in the cities, however, were not so well-off, and wages hardly rose fast enough to keep up with inflation in the urban areas.

From the British point of view, the rigours of keeping control over this troublesome possession paid dividends during the war. The strategic motives which had lain behind the decision to take control in the first place now showed their force. Palestine along with Egypt became a major base for British operations in the whole Middle East.

However, as far as the Palestinians and Zionists were concerned, whatever immediate economic benefits the war might have brought, nothing had been done to resolve the unequal conflict which a few years later was to leave some 700,000 Palestinians cut off from their homes and land.

The Zionists had, since the publication of the 1939 White Paper, made it increasingly clear that they sought not a 'national home' or an 'enclave' in Palestine, but an exclusively Jewish state. The Biltmore programme published in the United States in 1943 made this point clear.

When the war in Europe was over, they launched a struggle to this end inside Palestine as well as abroad. Hostilities were now directed mainly against the British who no longer appeared as protectors but as the chief obstacle to Zionist goals.

The British had lost effective control over much of the country by 1947 and clashes also escalated between the Haganah, other Zionist paramilitary groups like Irgun and the Stern Gang, and groups of Palestinian guerrillas, some of which received support from neighbouring Arab states.

When it became clear that the British, debilitated by the war and preoccupied with problems elsewhere, would finally quit Palestine altogether, both sides tried to establish control over key areas.

It seems clear from evidence which has emerged that during the 1947-48 period Zionist forces deliberately attempted, by intimidation and propaganda as well as by physical force, to 'encourage' Palestinians to flee their homes, particularly in urban areas and on the coastal plain.

The Palestinians' own political and military organisation was far less effective – the nationalist movement and its leadership had not recovered from the weakening effects of final defeat by the British in the rebellion and the internal splits which that struggle had thrown up.

Daily life became more than ever tangled up with political and military struggles and the economic gains which some sections of the Palestinian population had made during the war could not be consolidated. The post war period was a prelude to the breakup in 1948-49 of Palestinian society.

Where people ended up and under what social and economic conditions was partly a matter of the chances of war and partly depended on their previous lives. Obviously those with either portable wealth which they managed to salvage or the asset of education tended to fare better than those who were poor, illiterate or depended on assets like land which they lost.

Dispersion has also added new forms of differentiation, but whatever people's status, the memory of a land and society lost has been a powerful factor in creating the present determination to see statehood and land restored.

Claims to a state for the Palestinians rest on the fact that before 1948 they had land, a society and a culture of which they were forcibly dispossessed. In these circumstances, there is certainly a tendency to romanticise a past which has significant bearing on the present, but scarcely justifies the opposing view that the existence of such a society is a myth created for political convenience. In fact the counter myth, very much a matter of political (and cultural) convenience, is that the Palestinians 'do not exist'; that Palestine was an 'empty land'; or simply – in a common colonialist view of lands they wished to acquire – that the people there were just a few thousand ragged natives without culture or organisation who did not 'count'. This perspective has long been propagated – in words and photographs and at varying levels of sophistication – by Zionists, British and other westerners and has been used as ammunition in denying Palestinians their past and, by implication, their future.

43

Palestinians fighting in Jerusalem (probably in 1948). An old woman, with the insignia of a sergeant in the Arab civil guard on her coat, fights alongside the men.

Photographic credits

Introduction
1. Collection of Eric Matson, held in the Library of Congress, Washington, by permission of the Trustees of the Matson Collection, El Hambra, California (hereafter Matson Collection).
2. Collection of the Jerusalem and Middle East Church Association, formerly the Jerusalem and East Mission, held by the Private Papers Archive, Middle East Centre, St Antony's College, Oxford (hereafter Jerusalem and East Mission).
3-7. Jerusalem and East Mission
8-9. Underwood and Underwood
10. British Museum, Bonfils photograph
11-12. Quaker Girls School Collection, Ramalla
13-14. Jerusalem and East Mission
15. Matson Collection
16. Tamari family, Ramalla
17. Jerusalem and East Mission
18. Tamari family
19. Matson Collection
20. Jerusalem and East Mission (Estelle Blyth Collection), Bonfils photograph
21. British Official Copyright, by permission of the Trustees of the Imperial War Museum
22. Jerusalem and East Mission (Bishop Blyth Collection)
23. Pollock Collection, Middle East Centre, Oxford

Chapter 1
1. Jerusalem and East Mission
2. Owen Tweedy Collection, Middle East Centre, Oxford
3. Bowman Collection, Middle East Centre, Oxford
4. Jerusalem and East Mission
5. Owen Tweedy Collection, Middle East Centre, Oxford
6. Matson Collection
7. Crown Copyright, Royal Air Force
8. Matson Collection
9. Crown Copyright, Royal Air Force
10. Matson Collection
11. Bowman Collection, Middle East Centre, Oxford
12. B.B.C. Hulton Picture Library
13. Matson Collection
14-16. Jerusalem and East Mission
17. Matson Collection
18. American Colony, Jerusalem (Jerusalem and East Mission)
19. Tamari family
20. Jerusalem and East Mission
21. Tamari family
22. Matson Collection
23-24. Jerusalem and East Mission
25-26. Matson Collection
27-29. Jerusalem and East Mission
30-33. Matson Collection
34. Bowman Collection, Middle East Centre, Oxford
35. Matson Collection
36. Jerusalem and East Mission
37. Matson Collection
38-40. Jerusalem and East Mission
41. B.B.C. Hulton Picture Library
42. Jerusalem and East Mission
43. Matson Collection
44-45. Jerusalem and East Mission
46-47. Matson Collection
48. American Colony, Jerusalem (Jerusalem and East Mission)
49. Jerusalem and East Mission
50. B.B.C. Hulton Picture Library
51-52. Jerusalem and East Mission
53-59. Matson Collection
60. Jerusalem and East Mission
61. Pollock Collection, Middle East Centre, Oxford
62. Jerusalem and East Mission
63. Popperphoto, London
64. Matson Collection
65. Tamari family
66-67. Jerusalem and East Mission

Chapter 2
1. MacGillivray Collection, Middle East Centre, Oxford
2. Abboushi family, Jenin
3-10. Bowman Collection, Middle East Centre, Oxford
11-13. Matson Collection

Chapter 3
1. Jerusalem and East Mission
2. Popperphoto, London
3-8. Jerusalem and East Mission

Chapter 4
1-2. Matson Collection
3. Jerusalem and East Mission (Estelle Blyth Collection)
4. MacGillivray Collection, Middle East Centre, Oxford
5. Matson Collection
6. Jerusalem and East Mission
7. Israel Government Press Office (Klugel Archive), Tel Aviv
8-9. Matson Collection
10. Israel Government Press Office (Klugel Archive), Tel Aviv
11-13. Jerusalem and East Mission
14-15. Matson Collection
16. Webb Collection, Middle East Centre, Oxford

Chapter 5
1. American Colony, Jerusalem (Jerusalem and East Mission)
2. George Adam Smith Collection, Middle East Centre, Oxford
3. Middle East Centre Collection, Oxford
4. Israel Government Press Office (Klugel Archive), Tel Aviv
5. B.B.C. Hulton Picture Library
6. American Colony, Jerusalem (Jerusalem and East Mission)
7. Matson Collection
8. Jerusalem and East Mission (Estelle Blyth Collection)
9. Matson Collection
10. Jerusalem and East Mission
11-12. Matson Collection
13. Jerusalem and East Mission (Estelle Blyth Collection)
14. Bowman Collection, Middle East Centre, Oxford
15-17. Matson Collection
18. Israel Government Press Office (Klugel Archive), Tel Aviv
19-21. Matson Collection
22. Israel Government Press Office (Klugel Archive), Tel Aviv
23-27. Matson Collection
28. American Colony, Jerusalem (Jerusalem and East Mission)
29. Jerusalem and East Mission
30-31. Matson Collection
32. George Adam Smith Collection, Middle East Centre, Oxford
33. Jerusalem and East Mission
34. Pollock Collection, Middle East Centre, Oxford
35. Jerusalem and East Mission
36. Fox Photos, London
37. Jerusalem and East Mission
38. Fox Photos, London
39-41. Jerusalem and East Mission
42. Matson Collection
43. Jerusalem and East Mission
44. Matson Collection
45-46. Israel Government Press Office (Klugel Archive), Tel Aviv
47. Popperphoto, London

Chapter 6
1. Jerusalem and East Mission

2. Popperphoto, London
3-4. Matson Collection
5. Jerusalem and East Mission
(Estelle Blyth Collection)
6-7. Jerusalem and East Mission
8. Fox Photos, London
9. Tamari family
10-11. Jerusalem and East Mission
12. American Colony, Jerusalem
(Jerusalem and East Mission)
13. Jerusalem and East Mission
14-15. Matson Collection
16. Jerusalem and East Mission
17. Matson Collection
18-20. Abboushi family
21. Azouka family, Jenin
22. Monroe Collection, Middle East
Centre, Oxford
23. Asir family, Jenin
24. Tamari family
25-26. Mansur family, Ramalla
27-28. Quaker Girls School Collection,
Ramalla

29. Jerusalem and East Mission
30. Jerusalem and East Mission
(Estelle Blyth Collection)
31. Quaker Girls School Collection,
Ramalla

Chapter 7
1-2. Matson Collection
3. Jerusalem and East Mission
4. Abboushi family
5. Matson Collection
6-12. Jerusalem and East Mission
(Estelle Blyth Collection)
13. Abdul Hadi family
14. British Official Copyright, by
permission of the Trustees of the
Imperial War Museum
15-16. Matson Collection
17. Jerusalem and East Mission
18. Israel Government Press Office
(Klugel Archive), Tel Aviv
19. B.B.C. Hulton Picture Library
20. Daily Telegraph, London

21. Matson Collection
22. Jerusalem and East Mission
23. Matson Collection
24. Jerusalem and East Mission
25. Matson Collection
26-27. Jerusalem and East Mission
28. Israel Government Press Office
(Klugel Archive), Tel Aviv
29. Pollock Collection, Middle East
Centre, Oxford
30-32. Tamari family
33. Pollock Collection, Middle East
Centre, Oxford
34. Matson Collection
35. Popperphoto, London
36-37. Pollock Collection, Middle East
Centre, Oxford
38. Matson Collection
39-40. Popperphoto, London
41. MacGillivray Collection, Middle
East Centre, Oxford
42. Matson Collection
43. Popperphoto, London

Bibliography

Books and articles referred to:

ABU LUGHOD, J.
'The Demographic Transformation of Palestine' in
I. Abu Lughod (ed), *The Transformation of Palestine*
(Evanston, 1971), pp. 139-64

AMIRAN, D. K. H.
'The Pattern of Settlement in Palestine' *Israel
Exploration Journal*, Vol. 3, 1953, pp. 192-209

ARAB CHAMBERS OF COMMERCE
Directory of Arab Trade, Industry, Crafts and Professions
(Jerusalem, 1938)

ASHKENAZI, T.
Tribus semi-nomades de la Palestine du nord (Paris, 1938)

BAEDEKER, K.
Palestine et Syrie: manuel de voyageur (Paris, Leipzig,
1912)

BARBOUR, N.
Nisi Dominus (London, 1946)

BERGER, J.
Ways of Seeing (Harmondsworth, 1972)
and J. MOHR
A Seventh Man (Harmondsworth, 1975)

CANAAN, T.
Muhammadan Saints and Sanctuaries in Palestine (London,
1927)

COOK, T.
Travellers' Handbook to Palestine and Syria (new edition,
revised by H. C. Luke) (London, 1924)

CROWFOOT, G. M. AND L. BALDENSPERGER
*From Cedar to Hyssop: a study in the folklore of plants in
Palestine* (London, etc., 1932)

FIRESTONE, Y.
'Crop-sharing economics in Mandatory Palestine'
Middle East Studies Vol. 2 No. 1 pp. 3-23: Vol. 2 No. 2
pp. 175-94

GOODRICH FREER, A. M.
Arabs in Tent and Town (New York, 1924)

GRANQVIST, H.
Muslim Death and Burial (Helsingfors, 1965)
Marriage Conditions in a Palestinian Village (Helsingfors,
1931)

GRANT, E.
The People of Palestine (Philadelphia, 1921)

GREAT BRITAIN:
Naval Intelligence Division
Palestine and Transjordan (London, 1943)

Parliamentary Papers
*Diplomatic Reports on Trade and Finance; Reports from
HM Consuls on the Manufacturing and Commerce of their
Consular Districts: Jerusalem and Jaffa* (1872-1911)

Palestine Royal Commission *Report* Cmd 5479.
(London, 1937)

HIMADEH, S. B.
  The Economic Organisation of Palestine (Beirut, 1939)

HOPWOOD, D.
  The Russian Presence in Syria and Palestine 1843-1914
  (Oxford, 1969)

JAUSSEN, J.
  Coutumes Palestiniennes: Naplouse et son district (Paris,
  1927)

JEFFRIES, J. M. N.
  Palestine: the Reality (London, 1939)

KAYYALI, A. H.
  Palestine, a modern history (London, n.d.)

KENDALL, H. AND K. H. BARUTH
  *Village Development in Palestine during the British
  Mandate* (London, 1949)

KIERNAN, V. G.
  The Lords of Human Kind (Harmondsworth, 1972)

LAWRENCE, T. E.
  The Seven Pillars of Wisdom: A Triumph (London, 1935)
  The Letters of T. E. Lawrence of Arabia (ed. David
  Garnett) (London, 1964)

LESCH, A.
  *Arab Politics in Palestine 1917-39: the frustration of a
  nationalist movement* (Ithaca, London, 1979)

MACDONALD, G.
  Camera, Victorian Eyewitness (London, 1979)

MEHDI, M. R.
  A Palestine Chronicle (London, n.d.)

MOGANNAM, R. M.
  The Arab Woman and the Palestinian People (London,
  1937)

NEWTON, F.
  Fifty Years in Palestine (London, 1948)

NIMR, I.
  Ta'rikh Jabal Nablus wal-Balqa' Part II (Nablus, 1961)

OLIPHANT, L.
  Haifa or Life in Modern Palestine (Edinburgh, London,
  1886)

PALESTINE:
  Department of Customs, Excise and Trade:
  Palestine Commercial Bulletin, 1922-32
  Superintendent of the Census: *Census of Palestine 1931*
  2 vols. (Alexandria, 1933)

PALESTINE EXPLORATION FUND
  Survey of Western Palestine (London, 1885)

PHOTOGRAPHY WORKSHOP
  Photography/Politics I (London, 1980)

PORATH, Y.
  Emergence of the Palestinian-Arab National Movement
  Vol. I 1918-1929 (London, 1974); Vol. II 1929-1939
  (London, 1977)

SAID, E.
  Orientalism (London, 1978)
  The Question of Palestine (London, 1980).

SAYIGH, R.
  Palestinians: from Peasants to Revolutionaries (London,
  1979)

SMITH, B. J.
  'British economic policy in Palestine towards the
  development of the Jewish National Home 1920-1929.'
  D. Phil. thesis, (Oxford, 1978)

SONTAG, S.
  On Photography (Harmondsworth, 1972)

SYKES, C.
  Crossroads to Israel (London, 1965)

  Survey of Palestine
  Prepared in December 1945 and January 1946 for the
  information of the Anglo-American Committee of
  Inquiry. 2 vols. and supplement (Palestine, 1946)

TAQQU, R. L.
  'Arab Labour in Mandatory Palestine 1920-1948' Ph.D.
  thesis (Columbia, 1977)

TARTAKOV, G. M.
  'Who calls the snake charmer's tune?' *Bulletin of
  Concerned Asian Scholars*, Vol. II No. 2 1979, pp. 26-39

TIBAWI, A. L.
  Arab Education in Mandatory Palestine (London, 1956)

VERNEY, N. AND G. DAMBMANN
  *Les puissances étrangères dans le Levant en Syrie et en
  Palestine* (Paris, Lyons, 1900)

VESTER, B. S.
  Our Jerusalem (Garden City, New York, 1950)

Archives of the Middle East Centre, St Antony's College,
Oxford. Collections consulted: papers of Sir Charles Tegart;
Humphrey Bowman; Donald MacGillivray and the Jerusalem
and East Mission.